The
Company of
White Knights

Also by M. C. Mitchell
'*A Message to Mankind*, 1975, Regency Press, and contributions to Michael Williams' book, '*Supernatural Adventure*', Bossiney Books.
Articles in various magazines, notably 'Foresight', with such titles as:–
Rabies (a severe warning)
Reincarnation, or the return of a soul to Earth in order that new lessons may be learnt.
In Mortal Danger
Man's Dual Role (re the work we can perform during sleep operating in the fourth dimension)
The Reasons for the present state of tension between the nations of the world and the only way to bring about a relaxation of this tension.
Message to a friend who sees the time coming when two beloved horses must be put to sleep. (re the Animal Kingdom in the next world)
Autistic Children
Warning to those who are tempted to dabble in the black arts.
War is obsolete
The Loch Ness Monster
The false value set on human life by present day society
Karma, reap what you have sown
The manner in which those of God's children manifesting in female form on Earth have been abused throughout the ages.
Star wars
The real reason for the present situation in Poland (1982)

The
Company of
White Knights

M. C. Mitchell

The Book Guild Ltd
Sussex England

The Book Guild Ltd.
25 High Street,
Lewes, Sussex.

First published 1990
©M. C. Mitchell 1990
Set in Baskerville
Typesetting by Kudos Graphics
Horsham, West Sussex
Printed in Great Britain by
Antony Rowe Ltd.,
Chippenham, Wiltshire.

British Library Cataloguing in Publication
Mitchell, M. C. (Margaret Claire)
   The company of white knights
   1. Spiritualism. Communication
   I. Title
   133.93

ISBN 0 86332 468 1

CONTENTS

Poem   7
Sketch of Jacques   8
Preface by M. C. Mitchell   11
Introduction (as dictated by Jacques de la Court)   15

PART ONE   THE TRAINING OF A NOVICE

Chapter 1   My Tutors   23
Chapter 2   Quelling an Uprising   30
Chapter 3   My Guardian's Teaching   34
Chapter 4   An Attempt at Suicide   42
Chapter 5   Terrorists   47
Chapter 6   Explanations   54
Chapter 7   Attempting to Avert an Accident   63
Chapter 8   Rescue Work at a Fire   68
Chapter 9   Danger from an Armaments Factory   72
Chapter 10   Refugees in the Aftermath of Modern Warfare   74
Chapter 11   The Rescue of More Refugees   78
Chapter 12   Supporting War Casualties   80
Chapter 13   The Service of Dedication   88
Chapter 14   The Initiation Ceremony   93

PART TWO   AN INITIATED KNIGHT

Chapter 1   Preventing the Spread of Nuclear Technology   99
Chapter 2   Helping at an Avalanche   103
Chapter 3   A Flood   117
Chapter 4   Change of Heart in a Scientist   119
Chapter 5   Influencing a Town Council   121
Chapter 6   A Dying Man   123
Chapter 7   The Origins of the World   125
Chapter 8   Child Refugees   134
Chapter 9   The Attempt to Avoid War   138
Chapter 10   Foiling Mercentary Exploiters   144

Chapter 11   The Peace Conference   148
Chapter 12   Helping those who Maintain Law   155
Chapter 13   The Lessons to be Learned on the Battlefront   158
Chapter 14   Quelling a Mob   160
Chapter 15   Industrial Greed   163
Chapter 16   The Meeting of Two Statesmen   165

PART THREE   IN THE DARK REALMS

Chapter 1   Avarice Holds a Soul Fast   173
Chapter 2   Pride Holds a Soul Fast   176
Chapter 3   A Gambler's Hell   178

Epilogue   181

Linking Two Worlds

Silken showers break
Day's bright rays
Fracturing them to
Arch the sky
Linking hill with
Hill briefly as though
Angels needed to cross
From one side
To the other.
As the rainbow
Links hill to hill
So do you who
Act as messenger, link
Earth to Heaven by
Tuning your mind to mine.

(poem dictated inspirationally to M. C. Mitchell)

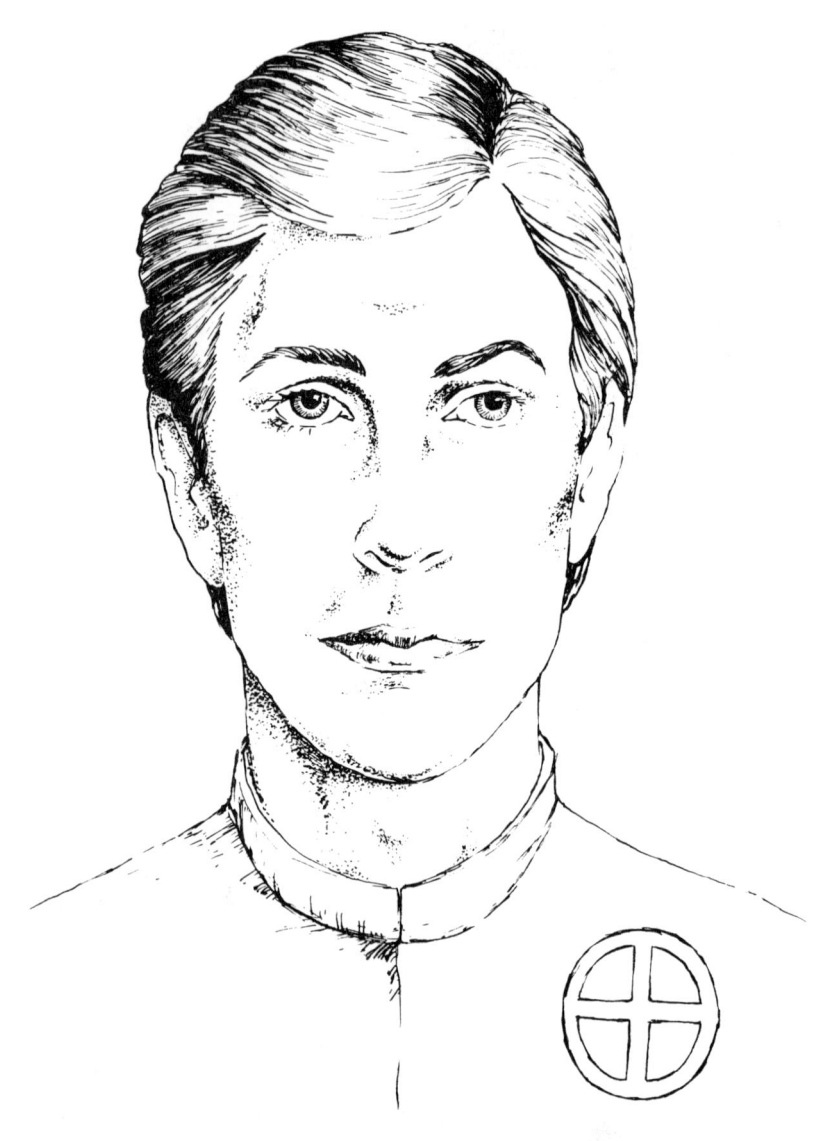

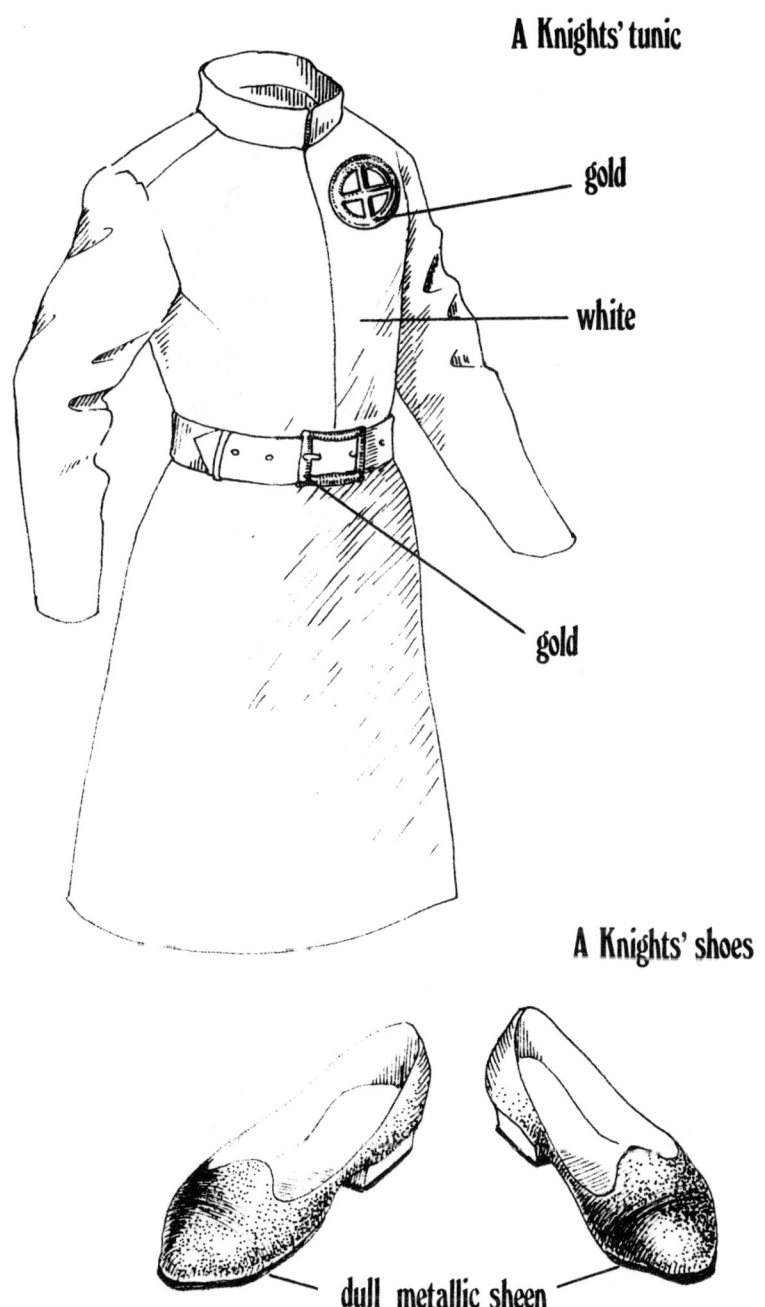

A Knights' tunic

gold

white

gold

A Knights' shoes

dull metallic sheen

PREFACE

In order to explain how this book came to be written I am writing a preface, for what has come to be a natural manner of communication between my incarnate mind and certain discarnate minds I realise by my friends' reactions is a remarkable fact and one which in some cases is regarded with suspicion if not disbelief, although they would probably be more ready to accept the fact that telepathic communication can and does take place between incarnate human beings.

In my own case it came about originally through my second husband urging me to try my hand at automatic writing in which he himself was particularly interested, and in fact his own father managed to write a few words through his son's hand. I should say here that we always preceded these weekly attempts, which were incidentally also attended by a young friend of ours, with prayers for our protection from any harmful, or even evil, entity, which we followed by prayers said aloud for anyone we knew to be in distress of any sort whether of a mental or physical nature. These prayers we went on to extend to hospitals and medical institutions on a worldwide basis including of course all their personnel.

When one day it came to my turn to take the pen and hold it over the paper in acquiescence to whomsoever of our discarnate friends might wish to attempt this (to them quite difficult) feat, I found to my astonishment that my late brother-in-law, my husband's elder brother, was writing in his own hand, which was quite unlike my own, being more the copper-plate type than my own, which was upright. 'Jack here,' he wrote, 'Jack Mitchell. Jack here.' It seemed too wonderful to be true, but next week he urged me to practise in between and not wait merely for our weekly sessions. This I did in solitude whether in my room or in the garden, always praying first for protection. Very soon Jack told me the reason why I had been told to practise and to strengthen the link between him and the friends who were backing him up. Some of these it turned out I had known myself during their last earthly lives if in some cases the contact had been brief; yet nevertheless it seemed in former lives we had had many close relationships.

What Jack told me was that I was to take down, through his help, a book* at the instigation of no less a person than St John the Baptist, who wished once more to prepare the way for his close friend, and in their last earthly lives, his cousin, Jesus of Nazareth, who had been set in charge of the welfare of mankind on Earth. He now wishes to draw closer to the human race by every means at his disposal for it is recognised in the heavenly hierarchy that man's hour of greatest trial is at hand. This is due to that force which is known on Earth as evil, now making its last desperate bid to create a state of anarchy followed closely by a nuclear holocaust of such proportion as would destroy humanity. This could alter the molecular reaction of Earth to the extent of which man is as yet totally unaware and which would in fact destroy the very planet itself; this has already taken place in other parts of the universe.

This close contact with the great Master Jesus would not obviate his physical appearance on Earth as has so often been forecast ever since his last life in Palestine; but rather he would seek closer links with peoples' minds and an insight into their problems. Thus he would have a means of speaking to their subconscious both waking and sleeping, and of passing on God's truths and His advice that they may avoid those pitfalls which are being dug for them by the evil ones at every stratum of society in this time of crisis in man's history.

The means whereby the two messengers of God, Jesus of Nazareth and John the Baptist as they are known today, plan to reach the hearts and minds of incarnate man are many, as for instance by the inspiration of preachers throughout the world regardless of their religious persuasion. It matters not how God reaches His children as long as His truths are being taught and the old superstitions of the past removed, as well as those dogmas which have been superimposed on the basic teachings and salient facts as pronounced by the great religious teachers of past eras. These are now revered almost as divinities although in fact they were highly evolved souls who had elected to return to Earth for the specific purpose of instructing less evolved mortals in the ways of God.

* A Message to Mankind.

Another way in which these two great souls intend to influence the minds of incarnate man is by linking telepathically with those who in former lives have practised the art of hearing discarnate entities, that they might pass on to their fellow men those precepts and practices laid down by God for the well-being of man during his earthly sojourn. These messengers might be in direct contact with God, or they might be in contact with those discarnate ones who had volunteered to act as Guides throughout the mortal life of one such messenger. All God's incarnate ones are accompanied by one or more Guides throughout their mortal lives. In earlier times in the history of man these messengers would be termed prophets, seers, Holy Ones; they were greatly revered and their words were taken down or learnt by rote and passed down to succeeding generations. Here there was always the danger of interpolations and misrepresentations which might tend to obscure the original teachings, and these distortions of the truth would always come about under the influence of the force of evil.

Nowadays these messengers from God are regarded by the major established religions with deep suspicion and anything they say or write is considered as heresy and not to be taken seriously; whilst those who do not belong to any established faith merely regard these messengers as eccentrics and again they do not take them seriously, although they would not consider them downright wicked as might the former category. It would appear therefore that the general assumption amongst those who consider the subject of world religions, is that such prophets or seers existed only in the past. The result is that anyone who claims to be in touch with more highly evolved beings in the present is liable to be discounted out of hand and their pronouncements or writings are liable to receive scant consideration. They are obliged to keep all they have learned to themselves, unless they are fortunate enough to find, through some far-sighted, less intolerant and less orthodox organisation, a means of presenting ideas to the public so that they may draw their own conclusions and formulate their own theories.

Returning to the subject of this book *The Company of White Knights,* here we have first-hand accounts of an initiate knight's experiences on the various missions on which he was sent, and before that as a novice knight. As discarnate beings they are sent to earthly situations where God's incarnate ones were in danger of a physical or moral nature. As a novice, this fine soul found himself largely concerned with rescue work of a physical character rather than with the work of counteracting the baleful influence of the force of evil who would ever lead incarnate man astray, causing him to break God's laws and thereby bring about certain harm if not total destruction to himself and to those about him. To those who consider that the moral welfare of mortal man is of primary importance rather than his physical well-being it should be remarked that in the eyes of God both conditions are of equal importance; for although it is true that man returns to Earth of his own free-will in order to learn certain specific lessons, in order to progress along the path of evolution, yet nevertheless it is of paramount importance that his physical well-being be maintained for otherwise it is unlikely that he will be in a fit state to master those lessons. Added to this it should be clearly understood that God does not countenance human suffering, nor would He wish to see any of His dear children endure the fear, pain and shock that accompanies a violent death whether it be due to accident, warfare or some natural disaster such as a hurricane. Thus it is that The Company of White Knights frequently have groups of its numbers sent to situations on Earth where mortal lives are in danger, for when under severe stress incarnate ones are often more able to hear the advice given them by discarnate ones who for their part are more able to see escape routes and courses of action that will lead to safety than are their incarnate fellow men.

In this short book we follow the many and varied adventures of a novice knight during his time of training, which was followed by the Service of Initiation as an accredited member of The Company of White Knights. The second half of the book describes his experiences as a fully accredited knight and this will be found to be of a rather different, more complex nature.

M. C. MITCHELL

INTRODUCTION
(as dictated by Jacques de la Court)

I have been bidden by those highly evolved spirits who direct
the operations of The Company of White Knights, to write, or
rather I should say, to dictate a book on the tasks allocated to
and performed by that select body of human beings, most of
whom are discarnate although some are still living, which is
known as The Company of White Knights. Our Leader is none
other than that great spirit known as Jesus of Nazareth, although
of course he had had other incarnations before that one for
which he became so famous for his expositions of God's Words
and of which we know so very little. (This is due to the
suppression of his own written work and also that of St John the
Baptist; and the distortions of the writings of their disciples and
their followers, so that only a small fraction of their original
teaching has been handed down to succeeding generations.)
Jesus it is who chooses which of God's children are to undergo
training in order that they may qualify as a member of the
Company, and it is he who decides when they are ready to be
admitted to the ranks of the Company having successfully
passed through their time of probation. It should be explained
that Jesus chooses not only Christians; the Knights of his
company are drawn from all nations of the world. Their religion
does not signify so long as they are true servants of God. In this
book I shall aim to show the way in which they are trained, and
the hazards to which they are exposed, the manner in which
they help one another and the initiation ceremony. Then I shall
devote several chapters to giving you some actual examples of
the varied situations with which they are confronted, and the
manner in which they contend with them.

Another aspect of the work undertaken by this band of tried
spirits is that of training others to step into their shoes when the
time comes for them to move on to other and even more
exacting work. I shall also attempt to show how The Company
of White Knights may be used to carry out God's commands not
only on this planet known to us as Earth, or *Terra* to some, but

also in the different planes of existence around Earth inhabited by those of us who no longer need to manifest in physical form, or who are merely having a rest between physical lives on Earth. It should be made quite clear that the methods we adopt are unlike any methods used upon the Earth plane, so that when for example we say that we do battle against the forces of darkness, that is to say those entities who choose to oppose the will of God, we do not mean that we set out to inflict bodily harm, nor any other sort of harm for that matter. We mean that we direct on them those electrical forces sent to us straight from God which render it impossible for these opposing entities to remain any longer where they were. The forces oblige them to desist from their work of destruction, bending their wills on the minds of men, or indeed upon the very planet itself. This will be explained later on in this book. Nor do we rely entirely upon these rays sent to us from God, for we are obliged to use the force of our own wills when we are engaged upon some mission which necessitates our overpowering the strong influences emanating from the evil ones.

So it will be seen that all those who undertake this work must first learn to control their own emotions of revulsion, anger, despair and any other negative reaction which may result from a close observation of some situation which is totally opposed to common decency and humanity. Not only must they be able to overcome their negative emotions, but they must also be able to concentrate their wills upon the task in hand quite regardless of the counter distractions which may be directed on them. These may take the form of most unearthly shrieks and howls (unheard by most human ears by the way) or the directing at them of foul epithets and blasphemies against God and His Holy Ones such as may scarcely be imagined by the normal person. Added to this there may be the deadening effect of the lower vibrations of electrical forces directed upon us, numbing our every sense so that if help were not speedily sent we should find ourselves entirely in their power. This may be hard for the average human being to understand, but the fact is that we all operate, or exist, on a certain wavelength according to God's will. That is to say, discarnate beings operate on a higher frequency than incarnate beings. Similarly with their surroundings, for we do not inhabit a sort of void! Our surroundings are much like Earthly surroundings except that here there is no corruption. But that is another story, and I wish to explain how it is that these heavier vibrations can cause us great discomfort, and even total immobility if they are allowed to continue. The fact is that these heavy vibrations can cause a disharmony within our own electrical circuits so that we begin to lose control of our movements, and eventually even our thoughts. How then do we overcome this powerful resistance? The answer is quite simple, although in reality it is quite difficult when it comes to the point. We have merely to send a prayer to those in control of our operation who in turn will then repeat it to God, and I may tell you that the response is instantaneous for a brilliant ray of light is directed on to the scene. This light is composed of an electrical force of a much higher vibration even that that upon which we operate, so that we must not enter within its circle. To our enemy it is as disturbing as was their heavy vibration to us, and if they have not managed to escape they are quite immobilised, as we ourselves were in danger of becoming had we not sent out a prayer for help. It is then that a chosen band of angels (who I must tell you come of a different order altogether from man) are sent to convey the evil ones who oppose God's will to that area where they rightly belong. To ensure that they may nevermore return to that particular place it is customary to cleanse the very ground itself which has been permeated by those lower vibrations which rendered it possible for the evil entities to operate there in the first place. We all know that such and such a place can have an evil atmosphere and can give any but the most insensitive of mortals an uncanny, eerie feeling as they approach it. These are the places where the concentration of evil power is greatest, but there are lesser concentrations of this power which may not be so easily observed by human beings; in fact wherever a person allows himself, or herself, to think or to act in a way which is contrary to God's laws, that is to say in a manner which is harmful to others, then that person is attracting to him- or herself the forces of evil in the direct ratio to the strength of the negative thoughts which they have admitted. n this context therefore, it is apparent that a close guard should be kept on all our thoughts, otherwise we are inviting the presence of the forces of evil, which are always on the look out to see an opportunity to influence our minds into taking the wrong course of action in whatever situation we may find ourselves. Similarly of course prayers to God will protect us from the evil ones, and with practice we should learn to hear His words of advice.

Having digressed in order to give this warning, I will continue with the introduction to the work of The Company of White Knights. It remains only to be said that they are drawn from every nationality and from every calling on Earth, and that their qualifications are a sincere desire to help the lot of man on his pilgrimage through the earthly lives which he is obliged to undergo for his spiritual evolution. They must also be prepared to accept orders and yet to use their own initiative upon occasion. These aspirants to the ranks of White Knights, or novices as they are generally called, may still be alive on Earth, or they may have dispensed with the physical body for a spell. Those who are still living in mortal flesh can be distinguished from their comrades by the trail of white light which lies behind them, sometimes referred to as the golden cord; this unites their sleeping physical body with the finer body in which they manifest during sleep, and indeed after death. (By the way, this finer body has none of the imperfections of the mortal body, so that if you have been unfortunate enough to have lost a leg, my friends, in sleep you will find you have its replica, and the same applies to any other part of your anatomy or indeed of your senses.) These incarnate comrades of ours, both male and female, are of inestimable value to us, for their close link with Earth conditions–that is through the bright cord which is in fact a form of electrical current flowing from the base of the head of the sleeping person to the identical spot on that person's finer, or astral body. This electrical circuit, in some way which I am not proficient to explain, enables us discarnate beings to draw closer to that human situation to which we have been sent than we could otherwise do. Unfortunately there are insufficient living mortals qualified for this work, on account of their ignorance of God's ways and His laws. Also, of course, they may visit us only in sleep, whether it be at night or a nap taken in daylight hours. However, this last factor matters less than you may suppose, for time in our dimension has no meaning in earthly terms. That is to say, should a person on Earth fall asleep in the heat of midday for a mere five minutes or so, his astral counterpart may accompany a group of us on some long and arduous mission which before it is fully accomplished may undergo many stages of development, many moves and countermoves of a most intricate nature before we either gain our objective or have to report the failure of our mission, (in which case other tactics will be evolved). But this daytime sleeper may awaken from his brief respite from Earth, finding only five minutes have elapsed since he closed his eyes. He may be dimly aware that much has taken place, attributing this sensation to a dream, or more probably he will remember nothing at all, so divorced is the subconscious from the conscious in the average human being.

The main point that I wish to make is that the services of an incarnate being are of inestimable value to us on account of their closeness to Earth's vibrations, for otherwise our higher rate of vibration makes it difficult for us to communicate our thoughts, (telepathically), into the minds of those to whom we have been sent.

This is indeed hard to understand; all that I can add is to ask you to accept my word for it.

Now that I have explained to you some of the difficulties with which we have to contend, I will tell you of some of the pleasures resulting from our work. These come from the satisfaction of seeing a danger averted, whether it be a moral one as for instance a man planning an underhand business deal, or some purely physical danger such as a motor accident. As you may imagine, there is no end to the possibilities and I can assure you there is no fear of boredom from the monotony of our work. In fact, we are astonished sometimes at the wide variety of situations to which we are sent. Later on in this book I will illustrate this statement by giving you examples of the work undertaken by us.

To conclude I merely wish to say that those who serve in The Company of White Knights are continually carrying out assignments as ordained by God, and that their efforts are unremitting in the struggle against the forces of darkness.

Jacques, a member of The Company of White Knights

PART

1

The Training of a Novice

1

My Tutors

In the first place his own spiritual Guides will tell him that our Leader has selected him to be trained as a candidate for The Company of White Knights. Here I should first explain that the candidate may be a spirit incarnating in male or female form, but for simplicity I will refer to our novice as a man. The fact of his having been selected will give cause for rejoicing and contragulations amongst his Guides and his friends. He will then report to the Citadel of the Company, and there will be welcomed by our Leader himself who will then explain to him, and to any other newcomers, the nature of the work they are to undertake, the qualities required in them, the pitfalls which lie before them, and above all their objective, which is to overcome the forces of evil and to prevent them from carrying out their work of destruction throughout this world. I shall tell you how I myself felt at this interview. At first I was filled with a great sense of pride to have been chosen by our wonderful Leader whose eyes shone with such love for us, inspiring us to do all within our power to please Him in these undertakings of such importance. But then, as He warned us of how our weakest points would become immediately apparent to the foe, I began to have my suspicion of doubt. I remembered then the warnings I had received from my Guides that I must learn to master my own shortcomings or I would be of little use to the Company, and in fact might even jeopardise my colleagues' chances of success, or even their own safety were I to fail them in any way. Seeing expressions of doubt on some of our faces, and sensing at once our trepidation, our great Leader then spoke words of reassurance. 'Do not doubt your own capabilities my dear ones,' He said, 'for I have watched your souls' progress carefully and I can assure you that you all have it within yourselves to master your weaknesses, whatever they may be. Furthermore, if you find yourselves in a situation which you find you are quite unable to handle, summon me and I shall come to your aid at once, for I would not have one of you in peril.' Then He smiled so that our hearts melted within us, and we knelt to receive His blessing. 'Go now,' He said as we rose to our feet again, 'and you will find that each one of you has his instructor or guardian.'

So saying He left us, and some of that beautiful light in that room where He had addressed us seemed to go with Him. We turned to leave by the way we had entered, our hearts too full for speech, and as soon as we reached the vestibule, or entrance hall, we were greeted each by his or her guardian who seemed to know directly to which one they should go. I was approached by a tall impressive figure whose costume suggested to me that he had once been a priest on Earth in the land of Egypt. This I found later to be true. Although his appearance was somewhat formidable his eyes smiled at me most kindly and gave me reassurance.

'My child, I understand that you wish to be known as Jacques, for you assume the form of that incarnation.'

'Yes, Master,' I replied, 'for my last incarnation on earth, though happy while it lasted, was short and ended in tragedy, and though I have returned to earth again, I lived but a few moments.'

'Nevertheless, my child, that brief renewal of contact with earthly conditions will prove to be of value to you. Moreover, it has strengthened the link, already strong, between you and the one who has been close to you through many incarnations, and would have been your sister in this last one, had you survived birth.' (And here, my beloved little scribe, he referred to you.) Whilst he spoke we paced slowly across an inner court of smooth green grass, and passing along what on Earth would be termed cloisters, although they appeared to be constructed of some finer material than rough textured stone, we entered his room. This confirmed my belief that my Guardian was an Egyptian of the ancient era, for it was furnished in the Egyptian style, and had murals and hieroglyphs upon the walls. In place of windows there were arches, or rather I should say massive pillars, squared and seeming to support the ceiling, and between these where one would in the western world expect glazed windows they were open to the world outside. Here were flourishing trees and shrubs of a most exotic nature, whilst beyond I glimpsed the shining expanse of a great river.

As I stood taking in my new surroundings, my Guardian seated himself in a most elaborate chair, whose arms were the representations of some beast; the feet of the chair were carved like an animal's feet or paws.

'Come, my child, seat yourself.' He motioned me to a stool set before him. 'We must become better acquainted you and I, for I am to be your adviser and, I hope too, your friend to whom you may turn when you find you are confronted by some difficult problem.'

I seated myself and looked into his penetrating eyes; they were set in a noble face, the cast of which was very different from my own, coming as he did of an ancient race, whilst I assumed that form which had lived in seventeenth century France. How strange, I thought to myself, that I should be taught by one who had lived so long before our Leader had founded the Christian faith upon Earth.

'You wonder how it is that I who come of a different religious order from your own should be cast in the role of tutor to you.'

I started perceptibly; then, seeing his understanding smile I answered, 'It occurred to me that our Leader is Christian, and you, o my Master, must have lived long before His time.'

'That is so. But the laws of God remain the same and will remain the same forevermore, and the laws as taught by the Priesthood when I lived and worked in the Temple were the same as those taught by your Leader, my son.'

'Forgive me, Master, but I know very little of your ancient Priesthood or of their religion.'

My Master then expounded to me the chief principles of his religion, which he then enlarged upon throughout my training as the occasion arose. Firstly he told me we must all accept the principle that although God rules over the whole universe yet even He must observe the law of freewill which must operate throughout the universe. And so, even though God sees people, His children, transgressing, He may not stop them. It is on account of this law, my Master explained, that all the ills of this world came about, and all its resulting sorrows, for had Satan, or Satanaku as my Master named him, obeyed God's will, then the human race would not have had to manifest in so material a form, vulnerable as it is to all forms of diseases, and liable to be injured in accidents. We were to have had bodies made of a finer substance which operated on nearly the same high rate as those used by us after the death of the physical body and during sleep. Moreover, there would have been no shortage of food, for these bodies would have been nourished by God's powerful electric rays. Reproduction would also have been by an entirely different manner with no risk or suffering to either mother or child. In fact, the child, or young spirit, would have been sent to those couples whose love for one another made them suitable parents, in a fully grown state. All this astonished me, and my teacher said to me, 'I think you have been given enough for the time being, my son. There is much more you will have to learn, but go now, for it is time you left on your first mission. You may come to see me whenever you wish.'

I thanked him and asked if I might know his name so that I might call on it. Kindly he laid his hand on my shoulder. 'You may call me Tetheera, for that was my name when I manifested on Earth in this form.'

He then directed me to the assembly point where I was to go and meet my colleagues, who were to accompany me on my first assignment. I felt elated and yet at the same time apprehensive. Would I come up to the expectations of those who had nominated me? How hard was the task in hand? My Master had made it perfectly plain to me that if I failed to play my part I would be making it all the harder for those who accompanied me. I hurried along the cloister–like corridor which had an open court and splashing fountain on one side and closed doors at intervals on the other, although I paid little attention to either of these, until I reached the central hall again where our Leader had addressed us. There I saw several groups of knights gathered, and distributed amongst them were novices like myself. I must tell you that although we all wore straight white tunics which reached to just below the knee, we novices wore no insignia on them, nor did we wear the jewelled belt of the initiate; ours were perfectly plain, having merely a golden buckle. How I longed for that great day when I might be counted one of their number!

'Jacques!' called a familiar voice, and there stood amongst a few other knights a well loved uncle of mine.

Here I must digress for a short note upon the personality in which I choose to manifest in this present time, for though I have the experiences of many lifetimes this one seems best suited for the work I am undertaking at present. As Jacques Delacourt I lived in France at the time of Louis XIV and often campaigned for that great yet sombre king. Although I have been to Earth twice since that time, both lives were of so short duration that I was unable to progress very far on the path of evolution. In fact, in my last life, which was in this present century, I scarcely had time to draw breath, whilst my poor mother also succumbed to the event, leaving her two little daughters motherless and my father broken-hearted. One of these little girls is she who now acts as my willing scribe; she was also my father, strange as it may seem to you, in that short intervening life spent in the English city of York. In that life in Louis XIV's France she was none other than my own darling wife, Madeleine. The uncle who called me by name had been my father's younger brother and we had campaigned together until that sad day when he died of his wounds, and it was I who had to bear these ill tidings home. Now here he stood looking quite splendid and in the prime of life again (as we all do of course on this dimension).

'Come here, my boy, for you are to be one of us.'

Great was my joy to learn this, and my fears fell away from me when I knew that once again I was to be comrade at arms with my uncle, although under very different circumstances. I hurried across the hall and embraced him, and told him how delighted I was to be serving under him again. His very presence reassured me and I felt that nothing could go wrong now; I had only to follow his example and all would be well. My uncle then took me round to meet our fellow comrades, and I must tll you that within myself I was astonished at the wide variety of types represented in our little band. To begin with there was a man from that part of the world which used to be known as Persia but which I understand is now known as Iran. He looked at me with great understanding in his deep-set black eyes as he greeted me and I felt that here was an ally on whom I could count. Next we came to a little lady from China, who gave me the impression of great inner strength but who presented outwardly a calm assurance that I found very delightful in so small and fragile a form. After her we encountered a man of medium height, whom I judged to come from West Africa as his skin was so very dark as to be almost black; and this I found out later to be correct. Again I sensed in him that same inner strength, this time coupled with a great good humour that I found most endearing. We very soon became firm friends. After him I was introduced to a very tall lady who, it turned out, came from that same city of York where I last spent a life on Earth, and where I was destined to die at an early age when giving birth to my first child. She too knew me although I now appeared before her as a man, and she embraced me warmly.

'I knew you too as Jacques,' she told me, 'for I was your groom and I accompanied your everywhere you went.'

My uncle laughed at my astonished face, saying, 'We are bound together throughout our mortal lives by the invisible link of love and affection, and though our relationships alter our love remains constant.'

He went on to explain how Rolfe my groom had accompanied me through many lifetimes in different capacities, and now we were to be comrades again. This time he had been advised to manifest in 'his' female personality as being of more service to the band of knights to which he had been sent.

After Susan, as I will have to name her, that being the name by which she was known in York, I met a gentle, looking little nun, who said she came from Spain. Finally we came to a large bearded man, who had the air of a pirate until he smiled, when his face took on a most benign appearance and I felt drawn to him at once. Here I should mention that the Spanish nun was also a novice, so I had the satisfaction of knowing that I was not alone; but I had hardly had time to take in the varying personalities of my new comrades before a voice spoke in my inner ear telling me it was time to prepare myself for my first mission. It was the voice of my Mentor. I could tell that my new friends had also received a message, for they all drew closer together, and my uncle, taking me by my arm, placed me between himself and that burly one I had described as looking like a pirate until he had smiled so warmly at me. He smiled again as though to reassure me, and I then observed that they were all turning to face outwards, and with my uncle's hand under my arm I did likewise. In this manner we formed a compact little group with our backs towards one another.

'Let us not be taken unawares,' my Uncle said to me in a low voice. I nodded, trying to suppress my emotions. I had little time for this, for we were suddenly enveloped in a soft yet vibrant light and I felt myself to be disembodied and unaware of my surroundings, nor could I see the forms of my comrades although I knew them to be close beside and almost touching me. This sensation, almost to be compared to a slight dizziness, lasted for only a very short time, it might be only a few seconds counted in Earth time, and then we seemed to become visible one to the other again. Immediately I saw my friends go into action and I myself received instructions, mentally you understand, to remain where I was and to concentrate my thoughts upon the support of my comrades.

2

Quelling an Uprising

I shall describe to you the scene which met our eyes. We found ourselves in a large hall, which might at one time have been used as a banqueting hall, but which now showed signs of disuse and decay. At the moment of our arrival, however, there were a number of people in it, and they were being addressed by one who was evidently their ringleader. He shouted at them in an excitable manner seeming bent on inciting them to rise up against those in a position of authority over them. It was at once apparent to me that this man who spoke so vehemently was being influenced by the forces of darkness, for I could see a malevolent – looking figure standing directly behind him, and by the intensity of its gaze it was obvious that it was directing its will upon that of the speaker, who remained completely unaware of the fact, as did his audience. I could also see other dark figures stationed at intervals about the hall, all with that same intent look which told of the evil thoughts they were implanting within the minds of the audience. My comrades had taken up their positions facing each one of these dark entities, and now it became a battle of wills and I concentrated upon my uncle and prayed to God that he might be made successful in overpowering his opponent. All this was carried out without the people in the hall being in the least aware of the drama being enacted so close to them. I then became aware that the heat had gone out of the speaker's voice, and that his audience no longer appeared to be so spellbound as before. There was a shuffling of feet and one or two voices seemed to be raised in protest. A man spoke, stating his views, and I could tell at once that they were much more moderate in nature, for he said,

'Come, Joska! There is no need to speak of murder and such dark deeds.'

At this point I must tell you that I received a message to go and stand behind this man and to pray that he might hear the will of God within his mind. I moved swiftly across and did as I was told. By now there were murmurs of support for him from different parts of the hall, drowning the speaker's retort. My man continued, 'Let me head a deputation to the mayor of our town, and I will put our case before him. He is a fair man and I do not think he is aware of these wrongs of which you speak.' There were cries of both assent and dissent from about the hall, and I continued to pray that God's will might be impressed upon this man's mind. Joska meantime seemed to have become quite deflated. He took out a handkerchief and mopped his brow as though overcome by heat, and the situation appeared to have lost its dangerous aspect, when suddenly I became aware that there were many more dark presences upon all sides than had been there when we first arrived. All this I was able to take in without relaxing my attention to the task allocated to me, and I realized that we were being heavily outnumbered. My uncle too must have realized this, for the very air seemed to have become charged with malevolence. (I was told later that this was because we were being bombarded by electrical forces of a lower vibration than those to which we were accustomed, lower even than those the mortals present were using, albeit involuntarily.) He sent out a prayer for help which we, the members of his band, could hear and evidently our opponents too, for they let out a most fearful cacophony of shrieks and cries of a most blood-curdling nature; and I may tell you it took all my willpower to enable me to hold my ground. But the response to my uncle's prayer, which he had directed to God, was immediate, for a wonderful flood of light instantly bathed the whole scene. The cries of the forces of dark which at first had been menacing and hostile now became anguished and filled with dismay. Where before they had encircled us, now their numbers were thinning out as with howls of rage they turned and fled, until only that one who stood behind the speaker remained.

'Go to your uncle,' a voice spoke in my ear 'Lend him your assistance by adding your will to his.'

This I did by moving to his side as I had so often done on the field of battle on Earth, but this time no feat of arms was required but an intense concentration as I directed my thoughts on the vanquishing of the malevolent entity before us. I said a quick prayer to God that I might not fail my colleagues and then gathered my strength to resist that beam of hate which seemed almost tangible. I had been warned not to look into the eyes of these creatures, for they were possessed of strange hypnotic powers, so I fastened my attention on the space above its head. Even so I began to feel my senses swim as a result of the unearthly force being directed on me. I pulled myself together and renewed my concentration. 'Go, go, opposer of God's will,' I said in my mind. 'Go, tormentor of mankind, and may they only hear His word.' In this way I managed to maintain a firm grip of my senses, and felt I had won a small battle of my own. At this point I saw that my colleagues had drawn close and that they too were focusing their attention on this powerful opponent. Apparently this was too much even for him, for he gave a most blood-curdling yell and seemed to disappear through the wall behind him. There was no pause for self congratulation, however, for no sooner had he gone than we were told to resume our places and I returned to the man by whom I had been stationed. Strange though it may seem to you, nothing appeared to have happened in Earth time whilst we had been engaged in vanquishing our enemy. My man was still talking in more reasonable terms, but now he seemed to have gained the sympathies of the audience, who turned and regarded him with looks of understanding and trust, occasionally interpolating words of assent until it became apparent that by mutual consent he had become their new ringleader. A deputation was formed from amongst their number and my friend appeared to be confident that he would obtain the reforms needed to improve their living conditions, and also certain outdated agreements in their working lives. During these discussions the man who had formerly been addressing them from the low platform at the end of the hall attempted from time to time to regain the ascendancy, but he was quite unable to do so. Eventually someone said good-humouredly, 'Come down, Joska, you have had your say.'

'Ah, you have changed your tune,' responded Joska, but without heat, for the wind had been taken out of his sails.

'We know you,' said somebody else, 'remember that time. . . .'

'Yes, yes, I know what you are going to say,' said Joska,

ambling down off the stage to argue with his friends.

Meantime, I had received instructions to join my fellows in a group at the back of the hall, and no sooner were we standing shoulder to shoulder than I experienced that same disembodied sensation that I felt before, and the next thing I knew I found myself back in the assembly Hall of the Citadel of the White Knights. My comrades all turned smiling faces upon me.

'Well done, Jacques,' they said, 'you played your part well. We know now we can count on your support. That was no easy initiation. That was a most powerful entity in charge of the opposition.'

At this point I noticed that my uncle had not returned with us, nor had Susan, whom I had known in my last life as nursemaid. I started in alarm.

'Where is my uncle?' I exclaimed. 'I must return to find him.'

But my new comrades assured me that he was perfectly all right, and that he and Susan had been instructed to remain with the deputising party until they had put forward their claims and had received just treatment. Having received this assurance I felt within me a sudden longing to visit my Guardian, for I wished to satisfy my mind on a number of points. I hesitated, not knowing whether we had to receive official dismissal. Then I heard a voice say to me, 'You may go now, your mission is completed. You have borne yourself well. You may report to your Guardian.'

3

My Guardian's Teaching

Smiling a farewell at one another our little band dispersed in different directions, and I made my way between the groups of knights out into the cloisters and there I hurried along until I reached my Master's door. This was unmistakable, for it had Egyptian motives on it, which I had noticed the first time he took me there. I was about to knock when it opened and there stood my Guardian smiling at me. 'Come in, my child,' he said, leading me kindly to my stool. There I sat with a feeling of comfort and relief to be back with him, my first mission accomplished. Moreover, I felt greatly reassured in his benign presence.

'I have received a good account of the way in which you bore yourself. The mission proved harder than was expected. Had it failed, the unrest might have spread to the proportion of a revolution, with the accompanying loss of life and limb. Now this has been averted.'

'Oh, my Master, I felt these people to have very real and just cause for grievance, but that they were being led astray by the one who addressed them.'

'Your judgement is correct and does you credit. At this moment your uncle and your friend are making sure that these people receive fair treatment. If they encounter difficulty you will be summoned once more to help.'

I felt a burst of pride to think that once more my presence might be needed. 'And now, is there anything you wish to ask, my child?' said my Guardian, Tetheera, smiling encouragement.

'Oh, there are many thing, I wish to ask,' I replied impetuously; 'to begin with, how is it that we are transported from the Hall where we must meet to the place where we are to carry out our assignment?'

'This is a highly skilled operation, which is carried out by those discarnate beings who have volunteered to be trained in the art, and who when living on Earth were generally possessed of those talents which best lend themselves to this work. In times past these talents may have lain in the field of construction work, or engineering even if it was only of a primitive nature (although in the days of Atlantis these people were far in advance of present-day technology in this sphere). In the present century, however, man has begun to master the electrical forces at his disposal, so that electronic engineers who come to us to carry out this work already have a fair grasp of what will be required of them. In this particular instance, they must learn to manipulate the electrical forces of the universe and to direct them where they are needed. To answer your question I must explain to you that all life, and indeed anything you care to mention within the universe, operates or exists on a certain wavelength; that is to say, all matter is in perpetual motion, although this is not apparent to the human eye either in this dimension or in the earthly one, for the rate is too fast to be observed. When it is ordained by God that beings on one dimension should operate or manifest upon another, these operators direct the necessary electrical currents on whomsoever it is, that the particles of which they are composed may be speeded up or slowed down, as the case may be, to allow them to be transported to the correct dimension. When this is done, their share of the work is completed, and another set of operators take over in order to effect the transportation of this person, or persons as the case may be, to the required location. These operators, as we will call them, will have received their orders from a higher order of being, who in turn will have had their instructions from God.'

'One thing puzzles me, o my Master,' I said, 'and that is that I saw none of these operators of whom you speak, either in the Hall of Assembly or at the scene of our encounter. Does this mean that they themselves are upon yet another dimension?'

'They are, indeed moreover; they can respond at once to directions given them from yet another dimension, that is to say from those highly evolved spirits who are in charge of the operation and who in turn act upon God's instructions. These highly evolved ones are those who speak into your mind telling you what to do whilst you are engaged on a mission. It is they who monitor the entire exercise, for they are viewing the situation as a whole and are able to see what action is necessary, better than you who are on the spot can. They are also able to tell if any member of the band, or indeed the whole band, is in danger of being overcome by the lower vibrations which their opponents are directing upon them. In the case of your recent mission they observed that your opponents had been reinforced and that your party was greatly outnumbered, so they spoke to your uncle, who is the Leader: 'Request help from God.' This he did, as you will have seen for yourself, and, my child, you may be confident that the response to such a request will be instantaneous. So you need never fear, for you will always be well protected.'

I thanked my Master for his lucid explanation, and went on to my next question, which was to ask how it was that he knew all about the mission from which I had only just returned. This, he said, was because those who had monitored us had made a report to him, as he had been put in charge of my training. He said, smiling as he spoke, that I had given a very good account of myself, especially when the most powerful opponent had directed the full force of the rays at his disposal on me (perceiving me to be a novice and therefore the more likely to be overcome), for then my colleagues would have had to relax their attention in order to support me. I felt my heart bursting with pride when he said this, for I remembered well the moment when my senses seemed to be reeling and I had had to pull myself together and pray to God that He would vanquish our enemy. I described this incident to my Master and he told me that my reaction could not have been better. He then gave me a short discourse on how best to withstand those lower vibrations used by the forces of evil against us, saying that to link one's mind with God was to call into play a protective shield of so high a vibration that the lower ones could not penetrate it.

'All thought consists of electrical impulses,' he told me. He gave me as an – example the case of a man who wished harm to his neighbour on account of an argument they had had over their boundary line. He sent out such malignant thoughts that the poor man sickened and died; but the evil that he had engendered within himself, by sending out these lower vibrations in the form of thought waves, drew to himself such powerful vibrations that his own health suffered. He became ill in mind and body, and finally went quite mad, and had to be removed from the property with which he was so obsessed. Moreover, his neighbour's house and land were sold on his death to a speculator, who at once erected a factory, there by destroying the value of this man's property. He added that once a person has given himself over to some evil undertaking he will find it extremely hard if not impossible to free himself from the influences of the forces of evil, for they will have 'tuned in' to his wavelength, so that they can continue to implant evil thoughts into his mind. I then asked if it were not possible for such a person to free himself by prayer, and was told, 'Yes indeed, if he has sufficient strength of will, but in most cases there is not the necessary driving force. The individual may require the support of others, and if possible someone versed in the art of freeing mortals from the influence of the forces of darkness.'

My Master then went on to tell me that the same principle applied to a place or a particular location on Earth, but that this could be freed from the heavier vibrations implanted there by a request for God's help, which would instantly be sent in the form of a higher rate of vibration being directed on to that area. He also said that it was better if at least one of those requesting help were incarnate beings for they, operating on Earth's vibrations, supplied the necessary link to create a circuit. I felt myself to be somewhat out of my depth at this point, and my Master, Tetheera, recognising this, at once said, 'It is harder for you who have not lived on Earth in this present era when the basic principles of electricity are common to most people. If you wish I will arrange for you to attend classes with one more qualified than I am to expatiate on them.'

I thanked him, saying that at present I was content to accept his word, but that if I felt the need to go further into the subject later on in my training I should accept his offer. At the present I felt I would rather concentrate my thoughts on what was required of me as a novice.

'I think that is a wise decision, my child,' he said, smiling at me 'meantime; continue to bear in mind that on all your missions your opponents' weapons are of this electrical nature, for they have none other, and even should they attempt to hypnotise you with their eyes (and I know you have been warned against this) they are redirecting the forces played upon them by those who command them.'

It was at this moment that I felt an overwhelming curiosity about these forces who dare to oppose God's will, and to bring such misery to the inhabitants of Earth.

'O my Master!' I exclaimed, 'who are these beings who set themselves against God's laws and seek to injure and lead astray His children? From whence do they come?'

'My child, you have touched upon one of the mysteries of the universe. Suffice it to say that they have always been present through all time, long before the creation of this world with which we are concerned at this stage of our evolution.'

'Then, O, my Master, even when we have banished them from one scene of action, they are likely merely to turn their attention to another. I can see no end to this perpetual state of warfare.'

My Master, Tetheera, looked very solemn as he answered, 'This is not our concern. We must accept the facts and continue to do our utmost to oppose them, out of loyalty both to God, and to our fellows living on Earth, who, because they cannot hear our words of warning, remain largely in ignorance of the perils which beset them on every hand. Those few who are able to hear us are largely disregarded or even treated as though they were mad, or at the worst as 'in league with the devil', at best as over imaginative.' He then added, 'In this modern era they are accused of listening to their own subconscious. It is as though they fear to recognise the truth.'

'This I can well understand,' I answered, 'for even in my last life I remember how such gifts as perceiving those who had died, "ghosts" as we called them, or hearing words spoken into the inner mind, foretelling events or giving warning of danger, were all much frowned upon, and considered to be highly undesirable.d I well remember my father having lengthy discussions with his friends and certain members of the clergy who were frequent visitors to our house, and if he had not been so popular a man as he was I believe he might have landed in disgrace. As it was he received severe reprimands upon occasions. The worst of it in their eyes, was that the information he passed on to others almost invariably proved to be right. My mother, too, a most practical person, and possessed of a serene personality, was undoubtedly what is nowadays termed a "psychic", although she seldom spoke of her experiences, being of a prudent nature. However, she confided to me, her daughter and close companion until I married, that she not only saw visitors from another world, but frequently held conversations with them. "I did not need to speak out loud," she said, "for I have found that they can hear my thoughts if directed to them. Otherwise people might say I was talking to myself," and we laughed together. I myself had some very strange experiences as a child, for we lived in a very old house in York, and at first I was unable to distinguish between its past occupants and its present. (I know now, that, some were visiting old scenes on account of happy memories, whilst others clung to their old environment out of ignorance of the situation, i.e. that they had left their mortal selves and should now leave Earth for a spell in yet another plane.) I soon learnt not to speak of these things to any but my parents and my nurse, for all others looked at me aghast or even scolded me for my "inventions".'

My Master nodded his head sagely. 'You appear to have a clear memory of your last life, my child, and I congratulate you.'

'My Guides recommended that I should cultivate my memory of that life, because they said that I would soon be working in close conjunction with those same people, although they would appear in very different guise. This I did, with their help.'

Again he nodded as if in complete agreement. 'Now, my child,' he said after a few brief moments of silence between us, 'I suggest that you go and bathe yourself in the waters of my pool, for in this way you will free yourself of the contaminating forces which have been directed upon you. I will come with you, for I myself may have been affected by them to some slight degree.'

As we stood up I realised the implication of his words, and I looked at him in some dismay.

'You mean that I have in some way brought something of harm to you?' I stammered.

'Do not concern yourself, my child, for it is of no consequence.' And he led the way down a few steps into his garden, which consisted of strangely exotic plants bearing brightly coloured flowers. I followed him along a stone pathway between these unusual shrubs and I noticed the air was full of aromatic scents. Turning a corner we came across the pool, which was surrounded by stone slabs and lay, serenely smooth, a foot or so below ground level. It was protected on all sides by tall reeds which I learnt later are called papyrus. Turning to me my Master said, 'This pool is the replica of one I had on Earth when I lived my life as Tetheera, as is all this,' and he waved his arm to include all the garden. 'It is composed of finer particles invisible to earthly eyes and yet identical in every respect except that it does not deteriorate with age or climatic conditions. It will remain here so long as I desire it, and you, my child, may come and use it directly after you return from a mission. In fact I strongly advise you to do so.'

I thanked him, and then we stepped down into the water and he told me to immerse myself totally. Here I should explain that it is not necessary to undress in these realms, because water is of a different quality and does not soak into one's clothing or leave any feeling of wetness afterwards, for the drops merely shake off one. So in this way I was able to cleanse both myself and my tunic at once. After I had swum the length of the pool once or twice I saw that the Master Tetheera had left it and was seated in a small stone temple at the far end. I joined him, and he continued to expound the duties of The White Knights. We were, he said, supposed to support one another to the very best of our ability, and if we found a situation beyond our control to report to our Leader, who would then decide what to do. This must be done telepathically, for at no point must we leave our post unless we received orders to do so. He also told me to remember at all times not to relax my concentration, for it was then that my opponents would take advantage of me by directing their own thought waves into my mind. Rather than allow this to happen, if I found myself quite unable to maintain it any longer I should request to be withdrawn from the scene for a brief respite and then to return when I felt myself refreshed. In this way I would not be setting my colleagues at risk, nor should I consider it in any sense a disgrace to retreat from the scene of action, because nearly every knight was obliged to do so from time to time. Indeed, he said, in many instances the undertaking is carried out in relays, for sometimes they may take years measured in Earth time. I was to remember this warning with gratitude on some of my subsequent missions when I felt myself quite unable to tolerate the pressures being brought to bear on me. Another sound piece of advice he gave me was to suggest that I linked myself with God, directly I arrived upon the scene of a new assignment. This need only take the form of a very brief prayer such as: 'Please help me to do your will, O, God,' or 'Please help me and my comrades to carry out your mission.' This he assured me would be perfectly adequate. In this way I would be protected from all harmful influences.

It was at this point that I received my second summons to join my colleagues in the Assembly Hall. My Master too appeared to have received a message, for he rose at the same time as I did and laying his hand kindly on my shoulder he said,

'Go now, my child, rejoin your friends and when you return from your mission you may come straight here before you report to me.'

So saying he led the way to the back of the little temple and up a narrow path between some tall trees and flowering shrubs through a narrow passageway, which I found took me direct into the cloisters again. There he left me, wishing me well, and I sped along to the Hall. I was conscious of other figures coming and going but my mind was set on joining my new friends as soon as possible. Directly I entered the Hall I saw them standing together not far away and I hurried towards them. I saw at once that my uncle was not there and Susan explained to me that he had not yet returned from his last mission and that she was taking his place as Leader. As we spoke we were joined by a newcomer, new that is to me but evidently known to the rest of the band, for they greeted him affectionately. He was a tall dark-skinned man whose origin must have been one of the African races, introduced to me as Nyomba. His smile was brilliant, and I felt I had great confidence in him. Once again we stood together, all facing outwards, and I closed my eyes as the slight feeling of dizziness came over me.

4

An Attempt at Suicide

Directly it passed I opened them, to find a very different scene from the last, for we were in a small room, poorly furnished, and I saw before me a young man who was seated on the side of his bed with his head in his hands in an attitude of utter dejection. It was immediately made clear to us why we had been sent there, for I heard a voice say to me, *'He is contemplating suicide. You must act fast to save him. Stand before him and pray that he may feel the warmth of God's love for he feels quite abandoned by both man and God.'*

I stationed myself directly in front of this poor young man, who struck me as being illfed and thinly dressed, and I prayed to the Almighty that He would send His love and reassurance to this unhappy child of His. As I prayed I felt a sensation of warmth about me and a soft light seemed to envelop the young man. He too felt it, of that I am certain, for the rigidity of his pose relaxed and he looked more at ease. My colleagues stood about him in attitudes of concentration, although I noticed that Susan and the Persian were not there. As though in answer to this observation, the voice spoke again *'Your friends have gone to try to bring help. Continue to pray, for he is desperate.'*

At this I reiterated my prayers on his behalf and continued to do so. After an unknown length of time that could have been seconds or it could have been hours, I became aware of voices from beyond the door. The young man must have heard them too, for suddenly he sprang up and rushing to the window he flung it open and scrambling onto the sill seemed about to launch himself into space. I stood aghast, for there seemed nothing I could do to deter him, parted as we were by our different dimensions. *'Tell him he will land on the spikes of the railings below and not be killed, only cruelly disabled,'* said my

Mentor. I sprang to his side and did my best to implant this message in him. He appeared to hesitate, and then a girl's voice spoke through the door, and at the same time there was a gentle tap on it.

'Jean,' she called, and I knew why I had been chosen for this mission, for she spoke French, my native tongue as Jacques. 'We are going to visit Grandmère. Will you come with us? She likes to see you.'

To my intense relief he put his feet back down on to the floor. 'Me? I am not fit to be seen,' he responded.

'What does that matter? Can we come in?'

'The door is not locked,' he replied. It opened, and in came a pale girl with a kindly face. She was accompanied by a youth, who could have been her brother.

'Why on earth do you have the window open? Isn't it cold enough already?' She closed and latched it firmly. Jean seemed to draw comfort from her presence and matter-of-fact approach.

'Come, brush your hair,' she said. 'Where is your coat?'

'I have pawned it,' he mumbled.

The girl started, then concealed her surprise. 'Never mind, you can wear an old one of Louis'.' The youth nodded his head, and she continued, 'You have been so silent all day we wondered what had hap-pened. . . if you were ill, so Maman sent us up to see. Things are bad then?'

Jean nodded, but said nothing.

'Come along, perhaps Grandmère will have some ideas for you.'

As they left the attic room I followed, and saw then that Susan and the Persian stood close beside the girl and boy who had intervened so opportunely. The voice then told me that the crisis was over and we could leave, explaining that the young man had half expected the police to come, for in desperation he had stolen some food. We regrouped ourselves and soon found that we had been transported back to the Assembly Hall. Again two members of our party were missing, and I was told that they were accompanying the young man to influence both him and those about him, so that the course of his life might be improved.

As soon as we were dismissed I hurried along to my Guardian, and then remembered his instructions. I was about to go down the passageway and immerse myself in his pool, when his door opened and he stood before me on his threshold.

'Come in, my child,' he said, holding open the door. 'There is no need for the cleansing waters of my pool this time, for you have not encountered the evil ones on this occasion, nor been contaminated by them. They were indeed instrumental in bringing about the circumstances which led to this young man's plight, and in forcing him to take desperate measures. They then allowed these to take their course, which undoubtedly they would have done had not you and your friends intervened.'

By now we were back in our usual places, I on my stool and he on his carved chair.

'O my Master, there is nevertheless something which concerns me deeply, and I should like your opinion on it. When the young man, Jean, sprang up from his bed was there nothing more I could have done to stop him from his intention to take his own life? I must tell you that I felt quite powerless to arrest his movement, and were it not for the girl's voice calling him by name he would undoubtedly have flung himself from the window. I can take no credit for our success.' I dropped my eyes despondently to the floor feeling myself to have been inadequate for the occasion. But my Guardian assured me that I need not reproach myself and that he had had a very good report on my share in the episode.

'You must not expect to meet with success every time,' he told me, 'for there is always the element of freewill to be taken into account. Your warning about the railings below caused him to hesitate sufficiently long for the girl to reach the door.'

'Ah! Then he did hear me,' I exclaimed.

'The strength of your emotions made it all the more likely that he would receive your thoughts. You did well, my child.' There was a warmth in his voice and I looked up and caught, it seemed to me, a look of pride and affection in his eyes. 'Go now and rest in my garden. I have arranged a couch for you. Later I will come and tell you more of what will be expected of you in your new work.' I thanked him, and after bowing, as was the custom of my era, I entered his garden and before long came upon his couch. This was constructed of a wooden frame with what appeared to me to be rushes woven across and across it, the head being raised to a comfortable height and again finished with animals' heads. They looked to me something like wolves. I lay down and almost at once a deliciously drowsy sensation came over me, and as I gazed up at the graceful fronds of some strange tree I felt myself drifting away into unconsciousness. How long this state lasted I have no idea, but when I opened my eyes the Master Tetheera stood looking down on me with a smile on his face.

'You feel refreshed now, my child,' he said, and indeed I felt a new being. Swinging my legs to the ground I replied,

'I do indeed, Master. Your couch has magic properties, for no sooner had I lain down on it than all about me became diffused and distant, and I lost consciousness.'

He smiled but said nothing, and seating himself beside me began teaching me again.

'You must understand, my child, that the forces who oppose God's will have no compunction in the manner in which they lead His children astray. Nor have they any loyalty whatsoever towards those whom they use as instruments in carrying out their work of destruction, for destroy they must, whether it be an entire planet or the life of a single being. Thus, if a man lend himself to their evil ways by cheating, lying, or in any way doing wrong to his fellows, sooner or later he himself will be caught up in the mesh of his own misdoings, whether in his present life or in some future one.' He paused for a moment and looked at me and I nodded, for my own Guides had taught me this. 'I see that you have been well instructed in the Law of Karma, as I would expect. But I wished you to be quite clear on the points I have just mentioned, for you should understand, my child, that the occasion may very well arise when you will be sent to the rescue of one of God's children (or it may be more than one) who has sunk to the lowest depths of degradation but who still has within a glimmer of conscience and shame at the result of his evil deeds. Now you yourself, my dear child, may at first feel such a strong sense of revulsion when you see what are the terrible results of his transgressions that your first reaction will be that he should be left to suffer the consequences, as suffer he certainly would when his masters had no further use for him. This natural sense of revulsion you must learn to control, for step by step this child of God must be brought back to His way, hard though the journey may be and bitter his experiences along the road.'

I listened with interest to this discourse and when he paused I asked,

'Am I to understand then that it is a part of our duties to protect those already committed to crime from being influenced into sinking even further?'

My Master turned to me looking pleased.

'Yes,' he said, 'I can see that I have an apt pupil.'

'Nevertheless,' I went on, 'I am not clear as to my exact role under these circumstances.'

'Your role will be to protect the wrong-doer's mind from any further suggestions put to him by the representatives of the forces of evil to whom he has been assigned. This you must do by prayers to God that your charge be linked with Him, so that his inner mind is unable to hear the instructions sent to him on a lower rate of vibration. Do not forget that you will continue to be monitored and your Mentors will tell you what to do.'

I found myself wondering what the circumstances might be which would make me feel I could abandon one of my fellow creatures to the terrible will of the forces of evil, some of whom I had already witnessed at their work. Once again my Master guessed my train of thought.

'Such circumstances may be hard for you to envisage,' he said, 'but I think you would understand were you to see helpless victims being tortured, or children being cruelly ill-used, or even an entire community brought to a wretched state of degradation and poverty without a semblance of the common decencies of life, and all through the greed or indifference of those who have it in their power to alter such circumstances.'

At mention of these terrible injustices, I had sprung to my feet taking a few quick paces back and forth before I was composed enough to sit down again. He laid a kindly hand on my shoulder and my agitation ceased.

'I see well what you mean, my Master, for these people must have allowed themselves to act as fiends, and I could feel little pity for them.'

'You will be helped by the example of your colleagues, as they in turn were helped when they were novices.' He stood up, saying, 'Now it is time for you to join your friends and go on another mission.'

I too had heard the summons telepathically, and bowing I thanked him for all he had done for me.

'May the Great One help you in your work, my child,' he said. 'You may leave through my room.'

5

Terrorists

I hurried up the garden path and through his antique room which seemed to me like a museum, and yet possessed of a certain vibrant quality even without his physical presence in it. I soon reached my comrades standing in their usual place in the Hall, nor was I last to arrive for directly afterwards I was overjoyed to see my uncle striding up to his place.

'Jacques mon brave,' he cried, clapping me on the shoulder, 'I have heard excellent accounts of you.'

My delight knew no bounds for I had always valued my uncle's praise beyond others, nor was it lightly given. I felt unable to speak. At that moment Susan joined us and it seemed our party was complete with the inclusion of Nyomba, for we were told to take our positions. When I reopened my eyes on sensing that we had reached our destination I was astonished to find that we were in a beautiful stretch of countryside on what appeared to be a lovely summer's day. I could see nothing amiss nor could I see any sign of human life. Almost at once however, I felt a sense of foreboding and my Mentor said to me, *'Go to the nearest tree and concentrate your mind on the object hidden between its roots. This is a battery operated mechanism designed to trigger off an explosive in the road beyond the hedge when a vehicle passes over it at a certain time. Your aim is to direct powerful electric thought waves into this mechanism in order to set at variance its own electrical circuits. At best you may be able to put it out of action altogether, or failing that make it go off before the vehicle passes over it. Your colleagues have gone to attempt to make the driver go another way. Direct your mind firstly upon the right side. This mechanism is crudely made and it is somewhat off centre; then slowly direct your thought to the front of it, that is to say the part nearest the road.'*

I knew which was meant by the right because I was standing

directly in front of the tree with my back to the road. Two of my colleagues were with me standing on either side of this curious object, turned towards it, but I soon forgot them and all else as I turned my full attention on my task. I have no idea in Earth time how long this continued. To me it seemed interminable, and I dare not relax my attention knowing it to be a matter of life and death. At last my Mentor said, *'Leave this place. Close your eyes and we will transport you.'*

I did as I was told and found myself in that strange dizzy state. My Mentor then said, *'Look about you and you will see a short incline leading up to some trees. Stand at the foot of the incline looking up it. Some children are going to come from those trees and we want you to prevent them going any further for there is still danger in the road. At least one of these children is psychic and we are going to try to make them see you. Stand with one hand up as if to bar the way, and point vehemently with the other towards your left. At the same time you may speak for some may hear even if they do not see you.'*

I had barely time to grasp the full horror of the situation before I saw the children running helter skelter down the hill towards me. I stood in their pathway holding up my right hand as if to halt them and stabbing at the air with my left forefinger towards the left. I saw now why I had been stationed at this point for there was a small track leading off that way. At the same time I spoke, 'Do not go any further for there is danger ahead.' To my intense relief they slowed down their headlong rush, 'you are safe on that little track,' I said continuing to point. A boy spoke.

'Come on, I'm going home this way,' and he turned off down the track. I do not think he had seen me, but I believe my words had made impact on his subconscious. Then I saw the child who was psychic. She had stopped dead in her tracks thereby causing two other children behind her to stumble and fall in a tangle laughing and complaining at her, but she stood stock still staring straight into my face, half afraid, half enthralled. She was about seven or eight years old.

'Listen to my words my darling,' I said, 'for there is great danger ahead. The road may blow up. Do not go that way.'

She nodded mutely, and began to move slowly to her right, still watching my face. I nodded encouragement, 'That's right, make the others go too.' But she seemed reluctant to take her eyes off me, and appeared too overcome to speak. All these

actions took only a few seconds in Earth time, and it was then
that events took a terrible turn for I suddenly realized that there
was a dark form overshadowing one of the boys. (By overshadowing I mean that its shape, which approximated to human
shape, seemed to engulf the child; I was still able to see him but
as though through smoke.) The boy gave a wild yell, and then
shouted, 'Race you to the crossroads!' The others looked startled
and hesitated, 'Come on your cissies', he shouted roughly,
pointing to the road. I stepped in front of him and as I moved I
said a quick prayer, 'Please help me God.' Then I turned my full
attention upon this dark entity, and said, 'In the name of God I
tell you to leave this child alone.' At the same moment a brilliant
light fell between us, and I saw the creature shudder and it let
out a fearful shriek and disappeared. I believe the little girl
heard it too, for she began to scream. But the creature had done
its work, and the children formed themselves into a line
preparing for their race. I heard my Mentor say, *'Pray that they
may be stopped,'* and this I did most fervently. It was my friend
who turned the tide for she continued to scream and they all
looked at her.

'Whatever is it Marianne?' they said, 'stop screaming and join
the race.'

'No, no', she sobbed, 'don't go,' but two of them took hold of
her and began to pull her back, whereupon she screamed even
louder. The boy who had appeared to hear me left the little
track and followed doubtfully.

'Help her', I said to him, 'she is right, there is danger on the
road.' Again I believe he heard me in some strange way for he
said,

'Leave her alone. She's right, the road is out of our way and
we should be home now.'

The older boy looked scornfully at him,

'Oh you're afraid I'll win', he taunted.

'Race you home then', was the quick response.

'No, I want to see if the army patrol will pass.'

The little girl had become more composed,
'You mustn't go that way!' she cried with some vehemence.
They looked at her startled. 'It's dangerous.'

'Dangerous! Why?' It was the big boy who spoke.

'He told me.'

'He! Who's he?' said one of the others.

'The man. The man in white.'

'What man? I didn't see any man', asked another. She looked round, and apparently could see me no longer. 'He was there. I saw him.'

'Where?'

'Just where you are', and she pointed to the big boy who now stood where I had first been placed. 'He smiled at me.'

The big boy laughed jeeringly, 'Oh you're seeing the fairies!'

'Did the fairy speak?' asked another child.

'Yes, he said there was danger on the road and we must go this way', and she pointed down the little track. 'Then I heard that awful yell and thought someone had been murdered', and she began to get agitated again.

'I only heard *you* yell', said the big boy.

'And that was murder!' cried some wag. They all laughed heartily and the tension relaxed. 'Come on, or we'll all be murdered for being so late', said the boy who could hear but not see me, and they all moved off down the track, chattering. I noticed Marianne cast a last look back over her shoulder and I waved, but she was unable to see me. I sent up a prayer of thanks. *'Well done',* said my Mentor, *'we will return you now to your former post.'*

I opened my eyes and found I was back under the tree. My two colleagues stood in attitudes of intense concentration and made no sign that they had noticed my arrival. *'Concentrate your attention upon the part nearest to you. You will see wires emerging, we want you to direct your thought on the short length visible so that no current can pass along them.'* This I did, praying that I might do it right.

The effort to concentrate was becoming almost intolerable when I heard my Mentor's voce.

'You may step back. Someone is going to take your place. Close your eyes we need you somewhere else.' I stepped back and before I shut my eyes saw Mieng Cheong as we called her, though I do not believe correctly for she always smiled indulgently when we tried to pronounce her name. She quickly took my place, and I found myself transported to the side of the road. On either side it stretched fairly straight while here and there trees met overhead. 'Look into the ditch beside you. There you will see those same wires protruding from the hedge. Coming along the road shortly will be a man on a bicycle. We want you to direct

his attention to these wires. He rides along here every day and should notice anything unusual. Go a few yards to your left.' I strode down the road and almost at once saw the man approaching slowly for it was slightly uphill. I stepped out and tried to stop him. He did not see me. *'Impress his mind',* I was told.

'Look on the right my friend', I said, 'under the hedge up the bank. Quickly! There is danger.' I felt my agitation mounting and tried to control it. 'Look on the bank to your right NOW', I commanded as he continued to ride all unheeding. Suddenly I saw his eyes light on it, and with an oath he swung his leg over the saddle and dismounted, approaching with caution. It was evident that he had seen the roughly concealed wires, and he then looked from them to the centre of the road which had been disturbed.

'Tell him to report it at once and to warn anyone else approaching that way.'

'Report this at once my friend', I said in the same commanding tones as had before reached his subconscious, 'and warn anyone else coming this way.' Obediently, as it seemed to me, he turned his bicycle round and rode quickly away.

'Stay where you are. A boy with some cows will come along shortly. Go to your right this time.' I went along the road to my right. It was a peaceful scene contrasting horribly with the potential violence which lay close at hand. I soon saw the foremost animals leading the herd at a slow pace. *'Stand in front of the cows. They will sense your presence and be afraid. We are going to allow the explosive to detonate. There is no one near.'*

I hurried to do as I was told, and stood astraddle in the centre of the road my arms outstretched to either side. The first animal hesitated, as though it saw me. 'Go back', I said, 'go back', using the tones I had heard farmers use. At the same time the boy, about fifty yards away, was urging them on and I redoubled my efforts. The foremost beasts turned uneasily from one side to the other, and some behind them began cropping the grass along the verge.

'Get on wi' you', shouted the boy, 'what's the matter with you!' and he whacked those nearest to him with a stick so that they stumbled into the cows ahead of them.

'Stop!' I shouted, 'there is danger ahead.' I doubt if he heard me, and then came an appalling roar from behind me and everything quivered and bent as though a blast of air passed over it, which it must have done though I could not feel it in my dimension. Then sticks and stones began to fall about us. The cattle were terrified and rushed in all directions at once some even trying to climb the banks on either side. I saw the boy scrambling up the nearest bank and through the hedge and knew that he was going to head them off from the scene of the explosion. *'Well done',* said my voice, *'you may join the others under the tree.'* This I did on foot, passing the devastation in the road which was such as would certainly have caused the death of anyone passing. I shuddered as I thought of the party of children and the cyclist. Negotiating the hedge presented no problems for I merely passed through it, operating as I was on a different plane. (My sister has just asked me whether I could feel the surface of the ground under my feet as I walked along. The answer is yes, I do feel the ground beneath my feet, but it is not the same ground as that on which you mortals stand for it is the astral replica which I feel. That had no bomb crater in it.)

My friends were assembled in a group all but my uncle and he joined us immediately. We grouped ourselves exchanging a few brief words as we did so. I heard my Mentor say, *'We are not returning you for there is more work for you to do.'* We next found ourselves in a little house where there were two men and a youth sitting at a table or work bench. They seemed to be engaged on some intricate looking mechanism, and I saw at once that they were being influenced by the evil ones for behind each was a dark form focussing its attention on the human in front of it. *'Stand where you are',* I was told, *'these men are manufacturing crude explosive devices. It is of no use merely vanquishing the evil ones for more will take their place. You are to pray that God will send His Angels to cleanse this place that no evil ones can enter it again.'* I turned my thoughts inward away from the scene before me and prayed as I had been told. I had seen my friends had been stationed at intervals round the room and had no doubt that they had received the same instructions. No sooner had I sent out my prayer than a brilliant light flooded the whole room and within it could be seen some figures clothed in white tunics somewhat like mine only rather longer. Their features were a little indistinct to me. I felt that they existed upon a different level from ours. Nevertheless, I gained the impression that here was a noble order of being, wholly dedicated to the will of God. As I watched them spellbound my Mentor spoke. *'You may leave now. Your share of the work is done.'* Before going on however, I must tell you that upon the instant of the arrival of God's Angels the dark forms overshadowing the humans drew back with the most unearthly shrieks and disappeared like smoke. The humans remained unaware of the drama that was taking place about them. Reopening my eyes I found myself back in the Assembly Hall and with cheery nods we dispersed and went our separate ways, I to my Master's pool where I quickly submerged myself in its refreshing waters.

6

Explanations

I soon retraced my steps along the pathway leading to my Master's quarters, wondering whether I ought to go round and knock on his door as being the more polite manner of entry rather than direct from his garden, when I saw his tall figure standing framed by the massive stone supports on either side of him.

'Come here, my child', and turning he led the way into his spacious room. I took my place before him as usual on the stool.

'You have done well, my child. I have received a good report from the Mentors. You have obeyed their every word and yet have shown initiative when the occasion arose. Both they and I are very pleased with you.' He smiled at me with affection. I cannot describe to you my feelings of pride and elation, and I felt a surge of self-confidence run through me where before I had felt insecure and unsure of my capabilities. The Master Tetheera spoke again.

'I should warn you, my child, that after a successful start such as yours has been, there is some danger of the novice, feeling over-confident and of taking steps he is not yet qualified to do alone. Also, he may tend to relax his first ardent determination to concentrate on the task in hand and allow his attention to wander. This weakness will immediately be seized upon by the forces opposing him and may endanger the outcome of the whole enterprise. You have to learn to make a nice balance between the use of your own judgement and a dependence on those in charge of the operation, whether it be your Mentor or your Leader on the spot. You, my child, have been accustomed to leading men, and this quality will stand you in good stead. 'At the same time,' he went on, 'you must learn to take orders from those more experienced than yourself.'

'I accept this, O my Master, for I was trained not only to give orders but also to take them from my superior officers.'

He inclined his head in response, and his eyes rested thoughtfully on me as though penetrating my very soul. At length he said, 'So far, my dear child, your missions have met with success, but I must warn you that this is far from being the case at all times, and you must prepare yourself for failure and for seeing the opposition claim victim after victim before your very eyes.' I nodded, thanking God within my heart that I had not had to watch those children destroyed by the callously laid explosive before my very eyes. I found myself shuddering at the thought. 'Nor must you allow yourself to become too distressed by the sights and sounds you will be called on to witness, tragic though they may be.'

Once again I felt as though he had read my thoughts, and much as I revered my Master this gave me an uneasy feeling. I asked, 'Do you read my thoughts, my Master?'

He smiled and answered, 'Your thoughts are your own property, rest assured. I merely follow the natural sequence of thought as it would occur to me.'

'In that case,' I said, 'it would seem that our minds run along parallel lines', and then wondered at my own temerity.

'That would not surprise me either,' he laughed, 'for this is not the first time we have met, nor is it the first time I have been your tutor.'

I looked at him in some astonishment. 'Forgive me, Master, but I am afraid I do not remember you. When and where was it that we last met?'

He looked at me intently as though deliberating on whether or not he should tell me. Finally he said, 'Have you ever heard of the once great continent of Atlantis?'

'When I lived on Earth certainly I had never heard of it, but since then my Guides have given me some instruction on the subject, for they told me that I myself had spent many lives there, and for this reason they wished me to know something of it.'

My Master nodded and said, 'You came to me as a neophyte at the Great Temple of Atlantis in its golden days, and later you became a Priest and trained others to follow in your steps. Then came the time when once again the forces of darkness gained the ascendancy. Atlantis was destroyed by the misuse of certain powers known at this present time in history as nuclear fission; and mankind for the most part lost the art of hearing God speaking into their inner minds, with dreadful consequences. Indeed they sank lower than ever before in the history of this planet, and they are only now beginning to climb out of the abyss created by their own wrongdoing, led astray as they had been by the powers of evil. Nevertheless, throughout this time of darkness there have always been those who have remained faithful to the law of God. Foreseeing the final calamity that was to overtake Atlantis they formed colonies in different parts of the world. The largest of these and the most highly successful was the land now known as Egypt, but then named Khemu, which meant 'new Mu'. Mu, or Lemuria, was that once great continent whose civilisation was the first to be destroyed by that same means as was Atlantis. There were other Atlantean colonies founded by God's true followers, and there are still traces of them to be found in South America. They are spoken of as the Peruvian Civilization. There were also settlements in North America, where the wandering tribes, whose descendants are now known as Red Indians, were greatly impressed by their teachings and their skills which were far in advance of their own. Red Indian tribal legends bear record to this day of the strangers who came from the East and brought with them many wonderful crafts, and, above all, who could tell them the wishes of the Great White Spirit. Much of their tribal lore in fact stemmed from the Atlantean colonists, although it has become altered and distorted with the passage of time, particularly as it was handed down by word of mouth, and through carved symbols which have now lost their original meaning entirely.' He paused, but I said nothing, for I found myself quite spellbound by all he said. 'There were indeed other smaller colonies, and these were situated on the land now known as Spain, and further North in what is now France, and further North still in those islands now known as Great Britain. They also penetrated into the continent of Asia, leaving traces of their unique culture in remote areas such as Tibet, Petra, the northern parts of China, and several islands in the Pacific, some of which have disappeared since, owing to volcanic action.

'The remains of these colonies have yet to be found by modern man; of those which have already been discovered, the true explanations of the signs and symbols which have been uncovered are not fully understood. When they are understood they will throw great light on the earliest history of man on Earth. It should also provide a warning to succeeding generations as to the dangers inherent in not only nuclear warfare but the hazards, resulting from the improper use of nuclear power, to all forms of life and indeed the very planet itself. It is for this reason chiefly that the powers of darkness have done all that they can to conceal these truths from mankind, for their ultimate aim is to bring about the destruction of man and if possible his dwelling place, Earth. And so they have used their considerable powers to hide these facts by every means at their disposal. In the first place, they will manipulate Earth's surface in such a way that what are commonly considered to be natural phenomena, such as earthquakes or volcanic eruptions, subsidences, fires and inundations, will destroy or hide the records left by these enlightened peoples. Next, wherever such evidence is still to be found they will take pains to influence the minds of those who find it in such a way as to see that they take any of the following courses: to destroy it considering it to be valueless; to sell it piecemeal so that its significance is lost; to denigrate its worth in the minds of those who consider it; or finally, if all other measures have failed, they will if possible cause friction and heated controversy to arise in connection with the discoveries so that the all-important message is clouded and liable to pass unnoticed.

'Where they have failed entirely to disguise the greatness of a past civilization is in Egypt; here the pyramids alone provide living proof not only of their superior knowledge and skills but also of an ordered, contented society, and one which was maintained for thousands of years, until corruption, starting with the priesthood, spread throughout the land and Egypt fell a prey to her enemies. This again', he added, 'was done at the instigation of the forces of darkness, who had long had designs on these flourishing peoples. The means by which they succeeded in doing this was by using certain of the less evolved mortals who offered themselves as novices for the priesthood, and then influencing their minds so that they turned away from God's Holy laws. This was a gradual process lasting over some hundreds of years, for the priestly tradition was a strong and hierarchical system, which made it extremely difficult for heretics to penetrate it. However, the ways of the evil ones are subtle. Little by little they managed to infiltrate those who could hear their word and would obey their will, albeit unknowingly. So that God's truths, and His precepts for man's manner of conducting his life in relation to God and his fellow man, were altered and finally distorted beyond all recognition. Eventually a corrupt society began to take the place of the well-ordered one. Certain of the priesthood adhered to the ways of God and taught them in secret, for otherwise they would have been persecuted and their number totally annihilated. They also had those ancient writings that had been handed down from generation to generation of High Priests which were records of the past history of man and of his downfall, first in Lemuria and then in Atlantis. Moreover they stated specifically the cause of the downfall of these two once great civilizations which, if publicized to the world today,' said the Master Tetheera with great solemnity and emphasis, 'might yet save man from a similar fate.'

'Oh, my Master!' I exclaimed, 'are these records still in existence, or have they vanished through age or the work of the evil ones?'

He looked at me, and then said, 'My child, there are such records still hidden in secret places on Earth.'

'Are they likely to be found in the near future?' I asked eagerly.

'It is not permitted that they should be found yet, for even though they would provide a warning to mankind, still they must be withheld on account of the formulae within them which could unleash powers even greater than those which modern man has discovered, and there is no doubt whatsoever that at this stage of man's evolution they would be misused, for the forces of darkness would do all within their power to see that they fell into the wrong hands. I tell you this so that you may appreciate the urgency of the situation now obtaining upon Earth, for this is the most important message for mankind to receive if he is to continue living on this planet. For his spiritual well-being the most important message is that of the everlasting love of God, who would shield His children from all harm, were it not that the universal law of free will requires that they should make their own decisions.'

He then went on to tell me that if I succeeded in qualifying as a member of The Company of White Knights it was intended that I should compile a book, firstly of my experiences as a novice, and secondly of those experienced as a Knight. This book, he said, I was to dictate to someone living on Earth who had learned to hear the words of discarnate beings such as I, and who was willing to give of his time in order that those living on Earth might know how God uses His tried and trusted servants to help and protect them from physical and moral danger at all times. He went on to say that no one had yet been found on Earth who was able to do this task, adding that it was better that it should be someone to whom I had been closely related in former lives as this would make it easier for us both to hear one another. Meantime I was to work at the preparation of this book for sooner or later someone would be found of that he was certain.

I listened to his words with growing astonishment, for my Guides had said nothing of this to me, and I had thought that my training would occupy my full attention, nor had it crossed my mind that I should be chosen to be one of those who provide a link between the incarnate and the discarnate worlds. I said nothing as I considered the idea, and I found that I was wholly captivated by the prospect. If only people knew what went on behind the scenes, I thought to myself, how very differently they would behave. Then, too, to know that we are always there to help them in every possible way that we can, would surely comfort them when they were confronted by some of the many problems that have to be faced on Earth. I felt a glow of satisfaction as I thought about it, and looking up saw my Master's eyes upon me.

'Oh, my Master, this is indeed surprising news, and yet the more I think about it the more I like it.'

He nodded agreement. 'I too, my child, for in this way the people living on Earth will come to realise that they are not alone in their struggles,for they have only to ask God for help and it will be sent. Should you require guidance you may always apply to me or to your own Guides. It is better to seek help if there is any point on which you are unsure, rather than to give a false impression which may not be easily eradicated.' So saying he dismissed me, advising me to return to my own home until summoned for my next sortie against the enemy.

I bowed my adieux, thanking him at the same time. Already I felt great affection for this noble man. Leaving his apartment I stood for a moment in the cloister, and then I thought of my beautiful home and upon the instant I found myself there, standing in the courtyard before the portico of the wide front door. I ran up the steps and into the large entrance hall, from which two flights of stairs led up to the next storey. Here I had lived as Jacques Delacourt, and here I had brought my darling little wife, Madeleine, after our marriage, and we had lived contentedly with our children until she had died of some mysterious ailment which I believe is nowadays known to be due to a condition of the blood causing it to clot, but for which in those days there was no remedy. Our house still stands on Earth, altered somewhat by succeeding generations, but the one to which I returned was its astral replica: that is to say, the house as it was first conceived and constructed according to the architect's design, and with no blemish nor signs of corrosion on it, for it is constructed of those finer particles which are not subject to the elements, as are houses on Earth.

In the hall I was delighted to find my two grandparents. They seemed to be awaiting me, and advancing from their usual places by the great fireplace (only there is no need for a fire in our world) they greeted me warmly. They had always given me the utmost support during that life we had shared, and I felt that they had come now to support me once again during this time of my training. My parents were both back on Earth, and these were my father's parents, whose home this had been also until the end of their days, for it was large enough to accommodate two or three families living independently if they wished.

Together we strolled into the garden and sat on a seat by the river, and I told them of my new experiences as a novice. Their eyes were bright, and I knew that they had had a good account of me from their adored younger son, my Uncle Pierre, although they said nothing. When I told them of the explosive buried beneath the road, my Grandfather exclaimed, 'Ah! – this dastardly behaviour! I have witnessed it myself. No regard whatsoever is paid to the young, nor to the innocent bypasser who may chance to set off these things. . . mines, we called them.' He got up, and walking away from us bent down, and picking up a stone threw it into the river. All was silent between us for a few moments. I should explain that my Grandfather had been back to Earth again since that life in seventeenth century France, and had fought in that war known as World War Two.

My Grandmother had not accompanied him in this life for she had been resting, following a short but adventurous life pioneering in North America as a man. However, she had been sent to support him in discarnate form, on account of their affinity for one another.

As he resumed his seat my Grandmother lent forward and patting him on the knee said, 'We must forget past tragedies, for Jacques is to write a book, and we are to help him compile it.'

'Oh that is splendid!' I exclaimed. 'I can think of no one better. Grandpère, do you remember how you used to help me with my compositions? And with my Latin translations? Monsieur Ybert did not wholly approve, but I think on account of his great respect for you he let it pass.' We all laughed, and then we discussed the form of the book I was to write until we had drawn several conclusions, and I felt altogether more confident.

My Grandmother turned to me and said, 'You may use the room I gave to you for a study when you brought your little Madeleine to live with us.' I remembered well how my Grandmother had vacated her petit salon, as she called it, saying I must have somewhere where I could sit with my wife away from the rest of the family, and there we spent many happy hours together. At the same time I could not help remembering the long sad years I had spent alone there, after her death. As usual my Grandmother sensed my mood. 'Have courage, Jacques, you have found her again, have you not?'

I looked at her in surprise.

'Why, didn't you know she was to have been your sister had you lived in this your last life, and had it not ended before it began?'

I sat still for a moment as I tried to take in this astonishing news. I could scarcely control my emotions. Why had I not been told before? My own Mother had not mentioned it to me. Perhaps she too had not known? But my Guides. . .they must have known, and yet they had left me in ignorance. Springing to my feet I exclaimed at last, 'I must go to her! She may be in difficulties:– these are terrible times on Earth.' Then the thought struck me, she might not still be alive. There had been a war and much loss of life. 'Is she still on Earth, Grandmère? Do you know?'

It was my Grandfather who answered, 'She is, and you may

visit her when your Guides think fit, but for the present you are to continue your training. Your Grandmère had forgotten that you had not been told, but it does not matter now.'

I turned to him. 'Why was I not told? I can see no reason.'

'It was considered better that you should be allowed to grow up in your new personality in this sphere we are now inhabiting, without being confused by the memory of past lives and their relationships. Now that you have become Jacques once again, naturally all these relationships have come uppermost in your consciousness.'

I looked at him and understood very well the wisdom of all he said. At the same time I longed to visit this sister who had been my wife in a former age. Again my Grandmother read my thoughts. 'Do not forget she will look different and that you may not recognise her,' she said.

I stood reconciling myself to this idea. 'Nevertheless, I know that there will be something about her which I shall know at once: her characteristic response to others. . .her humour. She cannot have lost that.'

My Grandmother smiled as though at some recollection, and my Grandfather said, 'I am told she still dances wherever she goes, directly she hears music.' We all laughed, for Madeleine's dancing feet had become a joke in our family.

'Then I shall know her by that alone', I said, and it was then that I heard the voice of my Mentor summoning me to the Assembly Hall for another mission. I embraced my Grand-parents, telling them I was to go on another mission; then, bowing low, I left them by the riverside.

As I walked up the shady avenue towards the house I thought of all my friends awaiting me in the Hall of Assembly and, at what seemed to me the next instant, I found myself there. There were the usual number there, with the exception of Nyumba, the black African. I found myself missing his friendly smile which had seemed very reassuring to a beginner like myself; but my Uncle was there, and that made up for everything. I told him I had come straight from his parents, but we were then told to group ourselves and we were speedily transported to the scene of our mission.

Attempting to Avert an Accident

When I opened my eyes I saw a strange sight. I seemed to be enclosed in a small box–like structure with four people sitting in it. I at once realised that it was travelling at great speed, great, that is to say, compared with the vehicles of my day. I had no time for further speculations, for I then received my instructions.

'Impress this man who is in control that he must slow down for he is heading for disaster and annihilation for all of them.'

I at once bent my mind to this task, having first sent out a quick prayer for help.

'Slow down, my friend, there is danger ahead.'

He seemed to take no notice whatsoever.

'Speak to his wife,' said my Mentor.

I at once turned my attention to her. 'Tell your husband to slow down.' I thought she had heard me, for she turned her head and seemed about to speak.

'She fears his retort. Try him again. Time is short.'

Again I spoke to him in my most commanding voice. 'Slow down or you will all be killed.'

To my immense surprise he slowed down and half turning said, 'What's that?'

'Nobody said anything', said one of his passengers' 'but I wish you wouldn't go so fast, Jack. You know we're coming to that bottleneck.'

'He is right', I interposed, 'there is danger ahead.'

'Oh it's all right, Father, I know the road,' said the man who drove, apparently not having heard my words.

'The danger is not yet past. Try again.' I was told.

'You MUST slow down,' I said to this reckless man. But he took not the slightest notice of me.

'Turn your attention to the engine. It lies in front of him. You may be

able to interfere with its electrical circuit.' I turned my full attention upon the shining metal in front of him, praying that the electricity might fail. At the next moment I became aware that the vehicle was swerving irrationally, and in another second it seemed to crumple before my eyes. Smoke, or maybe steam, shot up and I heard screams and cries, and then, as it finally turned on its side, a dreadful quiet. *'Leave it. There is nothing you can do. Their own Guides will take care of them. They are all dead. The car struck an oncoming vehicle, unseen at the bend on account of a large slow-moving vehicle on this side. Your friends were in these other two vehicles attempting to alter their speeds. We will return you. Close your eyes.'*

When I reopened, them it was to find myself in my Guardian's shady garden. I found myself to be shaking all over, and the cries of those unfortunate people still sounded in my ears. A moment later my Guardian stood before me, and kindly led me to his couch beneath the trees.

'Lie here, my child,' he said. 'You have sustained a shock, part physical, part mental.'

'Oh, my Master', I cried, 'I failed utterly to stop these people! That man! He was so obstinate. That vain, stupid man. He would not listen to me, nor to his own father.'

'Calm yourself, my child. You did all you could, as did your friends. He has paid for it with his life.'

'And with three other lives too!'I exclaimed bitterly.

'You must learn to accept failures as well as successes. Now lie down. I want you to rest for a while.' I did as he told me, and he placed his fingers on my brow, whereupon I immediately lost consciousness. When I regained it, I have no idea how long afterwards, the Master Tetheera stood smiling down upon me. I felt myself to be greatly refreshed, and I sat up. My Master, seating himself beside me began to teach me again.

'You must understand,' he said, 'that the more materialistic-ally, minded people are, the more difficult you will find it to penetrate their waking consciousness, for they will be concen-trating on matters of a purely materialistic nature and this will set up a barrier, by reason of their lower rate of vibration. There are, however, several courses of action for you to take in order to reach a materialistically-minded person. Firstly, adopt the direct approach. Take, for example, the man who is set upon avenging himself for some wrong, real or imaginary, and you have been sent to stop him. Say to him quite bluntly, 'If you do this you are going to suffer for it yourself.' Naturally you will be more explicit, for you will have been furnished with all particulars.If he continues to make plans for revenge you must then try to gain his attention another way. Speak to him as though you were a parent or teacher giving very definite orders. Part of his mind may still be conditioned to receiving instructions in this way, unless he spent a very rebellious youth, in which case you may have the opposite from the desired effect on him, and you must swiftly change your tactics yet again. Unless this is a very hardened character before you, there is certain to be some other person in his life whom he loves or reveres. Your Mentor will acquaint you with these facts, and you must then point out to him in clear and simple language that this person will suffer, or think the less of him, if he acts in such and such a way. If even these words do not reach his conscious mind you will then have only a last resort, and that is to cause by telepathic means some friend or relative to visit him, and to dissuade him from this project. If this friend or relative proves to be as hard to reach as he himself, then you are in difficulty and must immediately report the facts to your Mentor, who will advise you.' He paused, and I suddenly remembered the stubborn man who had caused the accident by driving too fast, thereby killing not only himself but his three passengers. I was aghast at the recollection of the tragedy.

'Oh, my Master,' I exclaimed, 'had I already known what you have just told me, do you think it would have been possible to have averted this terrible accident I have just witnessed?' (for the scene was still vivid in my mind).

'My child,' he said, in gentle tones, 'it is improbable that you could have reached his conscious mind in the time allotted to you. His is a very young soul with little earthly experience, and these souls can be very easily carried away by the thought uppermost in their minds, (in this case it was the pleasurable sensation of propelling his vehicle at a high speed) with little or no thought for the consequences. It had been hoped that your colleagues might have influenced the driver of the larger vehicle ahead of him so that he could have overtaken before the dangerous section of the road. Do not reproach yourself, my child, you gave as good an account of yourself as was possible under the circumstances.'

At this he stopped talking, and I felt he had come to an end. I then addressed my Master on a subject near to my heart.

'Mon Maître, whilst I was speaking to my Grandparents, my Grandmother acquainted me with the fact that the wife whom I loved so dearly in that same life, and whose death at a comparatively early age caused me such great sorrow, is now incarnating again upon Earth and was to have been my eldest sister had I lived. Is this indeed so?' I tried to disguise my eagerness, but without much success.

He turned to me smiling. 'My child, this is correct. You were to have supported one another in your search for God's truths, and if possible in their propagation to others still unacquainted with them. Your other sister's role was to champion the animal kingdom on Earth. Owing to the fragile nature of your mother's physical self, engineered no doubt by the powers of darkness, none of this has come about, although she who was once your wife is striving hard to learn God's Holy laws by whatever means she can, living as she does in a society which still views such investigations with mistrust and scepticism, if not open hostility.'

My heart jumped quite painfully, and I turned eagerly to the Master Tetheera. 'May I go and see her, O my Master?' The thought of my little Madeleine treading this lonely path was too much for me. I sprang up and stood before him, awaiting his answer.

'Indeed you may, my child, although you will not recognise the outward form of the wife you knew. Nevertheless, the spirit is the same, and by your close affinity you may perhaps help her in her search by speaking to her subconscious self, which may then transmit your message to her consciousness. Lead her in this way to those who can pass on instruction, or direct her mind to those books which may be of use. But do not be downcast where you fail in your endeavours. Besides this unending search of hers, she must conduct her normal life as wife and mother.'

For the moment I felt quite dashed, and I must confess my eagerness drained from me, leaving me in a state of utter desolation. I had not foreseen that she had become the wife of another man, and mother of his children. This was too much. I could not witness this. I said nothing, and remained standing irresolute before my Master. He read my thoughts, and taking me gently by the hand drew me back on to the seat.

'This is one of the hardest lessons mortal souls must learn,' he said. 'No man, nor woman for that matter, can possess another for all eternity. The close affinity will be there, yes, whatever the relationship or sex the other may be. If you go to see her in her earthly surroundings you must not think of her as your wife, but rather as the sister that God ordained you should have.' (Here it should be explained that, although it was God's will that I should be born into this certain family, and work in conjunction with my sister so that a better understanding of His Ways might come about on Earth, the forces of evil, who oppose His will at every opportunity, managed in some way to manipulate the circumstances of my birth so that neither I nor my Mother survived it. This is indeed hard for some people to accept, for they like to believe that God is omnipotent, overlooking the fact that there is within the universe a strong force, generally spoken of as the 'force of evil', which defies His edicts and which will go to any length whatsoever to make man himself defy them. In this case I am told that the fragility of my Mother was engineered by means of an inherited tendency to a certain physical weakness, which coupled with certain minor factors culminated in her death.) 'If you continue to regard her as your wife it is unlikely that you will be able to help her, for you will find yourself suffering from pangs of jealousy and a sense of betrayal, and these negative emotions will help neither of you.' So saying he stood up and patting me on the shoulder said kindly, 'You have it within you to undergo this further test. Moreover, the time will come when she shall be yours once more, whether in mortal or in astral guise.' At this I raised my head and gazed searchingly into his eyes. How could he know, I thought to myself. I did not speak but he supplied the answer. 'Where there is such great affection as exists between you, and has done for many lifetimes, mutual attraction will draw you to one another.' I wanted to pursue this subject, but then heard the voice of my Mentor summoning me for another mission.

Excusing myself I joined my friends in the Hall. There seemed to be more of us on this occasion, but I had time only to smile a greeting to the others before we were told to assemble ourselves in readiness.

8

Rescue Work at a Fire

Upon arrival I found to my astonishment that we appeared to be in the midst of some great conflagration. For an instant I felt a spasm of terror before I realised that it could not touch me in my present state of existence, and at the same moment my Mentor spoke. *'There is a boy trapped underneath a fallen beam. He is still living but will suffocate unless a rescuer reaches him soon. On your left is a fireman wearing a mask. Impress his mind to go forward two paces and then bend down and search on floor level.'*

I saw the man at once, and sending out a short prayer for help I stood close beside him saying, 'Go two steps forward and then search on the floor.' He carried a light which he moved from side to side, but the smoke was such that he could not have seen more than a few inches.

'Go forward two steps, my friend', I repeated, and oh how I longed to take the light out of his hand and show him the stricken boy.

'Control your thoughts,' commanded my Mentor, *'and concentrate on your task.'*

Once more I spoke in peremptory tones, and the man moved exactly as if he had heard me. 'Now look down on the floor,' I ordered. 'Shine your light before you.' Once again he obeyed.

'You have made contact,' said my Mentor. *'Do not lose it.'*

Again I spoke: 'Look under that fallen piece of wreckage'; again he responded. 'There is a boy lying there', I said. 'Look closer.' Suddenly I saw an urgency in his movements, and with what seemed to me amazing strength he gently moved the piece of wreckage and lifted the limp form of a child of about ten from beneath it.

'Good,' said my Mentor. *'Now move swiftly to your right and up a flight of stairs. They are already burning, but you are immune. At the*

top you will find a passage, and at the end are several people who are unable to go forward or back. If they knew it, a fireman's ladder is outside the window of the fourth door on your right, to rescue people from the rooftop. Speak to the girl. She may hear you.' I saw at once the one to whom I should speak, for there was a certain luminosity about her denoting spiritual quality as my Guides had told me. I strode up to her.

'Come with me. I will show you the way out. Take that door on your left.' At once she began to move.

'Where are you going?' the others cried. 'The smoke will kill you! You can't get down the stairs, they're blazing.' She hesitated.

'Do not listen to them,' I said; 'this door is your only chance. There is a ladder outside this room. Open this door, I say.' She moved almost as if spellbound and put her hand on the doorknob.

.'Come back!' they shouted to her. 'You will create a draught and that is the worst thing to do.'

Again I spoke urgently into her mind. Smoke was billowing along the passageway and the poor unfortunate people had begun to cough as it reached their lungs. 'Open that door!' I almost shouted at her. As though in a moment of utter recklessness she flung it open. The room was comparatively smoke free, and there could be seen quite plainly the rungs of a ladder. In an instant she turned, beckoning the others to her.

'Quick!' she shouted. 'We can get out, there's a ladder here!' Scarcely believing her they stumbled to her side and then on towards the window.

'Well done,' said my Mentor. *'Now go up onto the roof. Many are afraid to take the escape routes offered to them. You are to reassure them. Close your eyes. We will transport you.'*

The next moment I found myself amongst a group of people. One by one the firemen were helping them to safety, but I could see that much valuable time was being wasted by the reluctance of some to take the first step into what seemed to them to be sheer space without any footing. It was dark, and the light playing upon the scene dazzled and further alarmed them. I stood close to the parapet and spoke reassuring words to each one in turn, adapting my turn of phrase to the age or appearance of the one I was addressing. The firemen spoke with infinite compassion, and handled the frightened people with great skill and kindness. My admiration for them knew no bounds. '*Stand close to the firemen. They are tiring. We will direct new strength to them through you.*' I did as I was told, keeping close to each one in turn as he went about his arduous, and at times extremely dangerous, work. If one of them descended or ascended a ladder I accompanied him, for in my dimension I could occupy the same space as they occupied. Nor was it necessary, I found, to put my feet on the rungs of the ladder; electrical force bound us together, my Mentor told me. In this way I was able to transmit those revitalising electric currents needed to restore the strength of these brave men. Indeed, I heard one say to his comrade,

'I seem to have got my second wind, Bert.' (I believe this fire to have been somewhere in the Midlands of England.) This continued until I had treated all those engaged upon rescue work on the roof. Here I should say that all through this mission I became aware of my colleagues engaged on work similar as mine, but for the most part we worked singly, as directed by our Mentors.

Suddenly I heard my Mentor say, ' *You are to go to the basement of the building next door: a fireman is in danger of being overcome by the fumes seeping through from next door. He was told to make sure that no one was in there. Close your eyes.*' I did so and was transported to an entirely new scene. A light shone dimly from down a stairway, but the place was in almost total darkness. However, we who are in this dimension see in quite a different way, and so I was able to discern a groping figure in a far corner. Already his gait was unsteady. 'Tell him to get out quickly, he does not realise how badly affected he is. The fumes are coming through the basement ventilators.'

I wasted no time. 'Go back, my friend,' I said in peremptory tones, 'you are being overcome by fumes.' It seemed he had not anticipated this eventuality for the fire had not spread here yet, and he was not wearing his breathing apparatus. Still he stumbled on, shining his light and groping into corners.

'Go back, I say!' I cried in desperation. 'There is nobody here.' I seemed to make no impression on him. 'Turn round', I said, remembering my Guardian's words, 'speak as though a parent or teacher.' 'Walk towards that dim light. Go up those stairs before you.' And to my great joy this brave man obeyed my simple instructions. He moved as though he were in a dream. But my joy was short-lived, for partway up the stairs he stumbled and fell, and nothing I could do would rouse him.

' *You must go for help,* 'said my Mentor. ' *There is someone searching the upper part of the house. Close your eyes.*' I found myself in a bedroom where a fireman was hurriedly going through it with his light, to make sure no one remained. But the bed had obviously been hastily vacated. He turned to the door.

'Come quickly,' I told him. 'Your comrade is in trouble.' He seemed to hesitate. 'Go to the cellar. Be quick or you will be too late.'

' *The name is Tom*', said my Mentor.

'Tom is in danger. Go to Tom!' I said in my most urgent voice. He strode into the passage.

'Tom!' he called. 'There's no one up here. Where are you?' He paused to listen.

'Hurry up!' I almost shouted. 'Go down to the cellar.'

To my intense relief he hurried down the stairs, calling in an increasingly anxious voice. I was at his heels. 'Hurry, or he will die,' I said. At last he found him, and attempted to move his friend, shouting as he did so for help. It came, as he stumbled along the hallway carrying his friend across his back.

'Quick, oxygen!' I heard him say, and then my Mentor told me our work was done and we could return.

'That poor man, will he live?' I could not resist asking.

' *He may do so, if they're quick enough in giving treatment. You played your part well. Close your eyes.*' I did so but I retained the memory of that man doggedly searching the cellar unaware that he was being overcome by the fumes.

On our return I found myself standing beside my Uncle Pierre. Before I could speak he clapped me on the shoulder saying, 'Jacques, my boy, you are to be congratulated. I hear excellent accounts of your progress.'

I was delighted for I had always valued my Uncle's opinion. At the same time I felt puzzled, wondering how he could know so much about me as we seldom seemed to be working together.

'Who has told you this?' I asked him.

'I am leader of this band and as such your Mentors report to me on the progress of our latest novice. I anticipate that before long you will be promoted to your full status as a member of the Company.'

I felt myself to be overjoyed at this news and longed for that time to come. I then told him I had visited his parents at our old home, and we were discussing this when once again we were summoned to go on a mission.

9

Danger from an Armaments Factory

Upon arrival at the new scene we found ourselves within what appeared to me to be some vast piece of mechanism such as I had never seen before. I felt myself to be inside some great clock, although its different components were quite unfamiliar to me. *'You are inside a factory,'* said my Mentor. *'Here are made armaments of the most lethal sort man can devise. It is in danger of blowing up, due to an unsuspected fault which has developed. Nothing could be better, were it not for those who work here day and night and also for those who live in the vicinity. Join your colleagues who are standing by this fault and directing their full attention on it. You may then prevent its worsening before it is discovered.'* I hurried to the group of my friends who stood close by, and turned my attention upon the piece of machinery beside them. It appeared to me to be running smoothly enough, though I could not make head or tail of its function. *'Look down almost to the floor level, and you will see a small pipe has a connection where it changes direction. It is here at this point that the weakness occurs, and the pressure within it forces a slight amount of vapour to escape now and again. Direct your thoughts on this joint so that this vital piece of metal may be sustained by the power which you are transmitting. Your other friends have gone to impress the minds of those in charge.'*
I directed my concentration upon the area described to me, and prayed that I would be successful in my attempt to arrest disaster. I found it extremely difficult to focus my attention for any length of time upon this small piece of machinery, and I would far rather be told to take action of some sort. Time and again my Mentor spoke. *'You are letting your attention wander. Think only of your task.'* Each time I felt ashamed of myself knowing quite well he spoke truth. I had no idea of the passage of time, I only knew it seemed an interminable wait to me; but

at last I became aware that someone was approaching, and then a strange figure passed between me and the object of my concentration. This ungainly figure appeared to be dressed in a single garment, which covered his head as well, so that he looked at the world, as it were, through a window. I returned to my task of concentration before being chided, but I could not help hearing the voice of my Uncle.

'Go halfway along and examine the. . . ', and then followed some technicality which I could not assimilate, but the urgency of his tones were unmistakable. Suddenly this uncouth figure appeared once more within my line of vision.

'Bend down,' I heard my Uncle say, as though giving orders to his battalion. 'Make a thorough examination here. Be quick! There is danger.' I could scarcely believe my eyes when the man appeared to follow the instructions given him. All at once his movements quickened. I saw him fall to one knee and make a thorough examination of the part on which we were concentrating.

'*He has found it,*' said my Mentor, '*but you must continue with your concentration until the fault is corrected. He will sound the alarm first.*' So I was not yet to be released from my arduous task! I resumed my efforts to concentrate. This was made even more difficult now, on account of the scenes of frantic activity which ensued. More muffled figures came and went, and in fact I closed my eyes, for by now I had a mental image of the faulty part.

Eventually I was told, 'The danger is past. We are going to return you', and after the customary sensations of transition from one dimension to another I found myself back in the Assembly Hall. No sooner had we spoken a few words to one another than we were told to regroup as there was more work for us to do.

10

Refugees in the Aftermath of Modern Warfare

This time on arrival we found ourselves in a desolate scene for there seemed to be no sign of life, either human or animal, or even vegetation. I found myself wondering if this was what it was like on the moon, indeed if we *were* in fact on the moon. . . but almost at once I was told, ' *War has been waged over this territory, and the people who lived here have lost everything; even the land has been despoiled so that they have moved away rather than starve. There are, however, a few people left, who do not know which way to go to find help. We want you to lead them by impressing their minds as to the route they should take, and where they will be able to find water to sustain life. Go a short distance to your right. Some of them are sheltering in a bomb crater where they have spent the night.'* I did as I was told, and found a pitiful collection of these refugees huddled together for comfort. There was an old man, who appeared to me utterly dejected and without hope. There were also two younger women, a youth of about thirteen, and three children. One of the women carried a baby, and the poor little thing looked as if it were dying. 'Remind the man that he once hunted here-with his brother and a cousin, and that they found a small river. It is still running, though its course has been somewhat altered by the bombing.'

I stood directly before the old man as he sat leaning his head into his hands. 'You have been here before, my friend,' I said. 'You came here with your brother and a cousin when you were hunting one day.' To my surprise he looked up, as though he had heard me. What is more, his eyes appeared to meet mine. It was a most strange sensation.

' *These simple people are psychic. Moreover, they have eaten little for some days and so they are more likely to hear you, for the physical body has less hold on them. Remind him again.'*

'You have been here before when you hunted with your brother and a cousin,' I repeated.

He nodded his head.

'*Tell him they caught a small deer and took it back home.*'

I repeated this too, and to my utter amazement he answered me, speaking softly, almost as though to himself. (Here I should say that once the earthly world of men is left language presents no problem, for everyone can speak in his own mother tongue, whether to incarnate or to discarnate beings, and there is instant understanding of his speech. My Guides have told me that this wonderful telepathic communication takes place automatically, for by some process they were unable to explain, the mind translates the other's words as nearly as possible into the hearer's language.)

'I remember the day,' he said, 'we came against the will of our elders. . . .'

'You caught a deer,' I pressed home my advantage.

'Yes, fate was kind, even though we had disobeyed our elders, and they soon forgave us when they saw our prize.' I felt I was losing his attention as he lapsed into a reminiscent train of thought.

'You found a small river near here. Find it again, my friend. It is the last chance of survival for you and your friends.' This roused him, and he seemed to look at me again.

'*Tell him it is not far away in the direction of the sunrise.*'

'You must go to it now. Lead the others. It is only a short way towards where the sun rises.'

'Oh, I am spent. I can go no further.'

'You MUST go. You are the only one who has seen it. Go now. or they will all die.'

'Very well, I will attempt it', he said, scrambling to his feet.

Then the boy got up. 'Come along,' he urged the others. 'Grandpa is going to show us the way to the river.' He sprang up and helped the others to their feet, and suddenly I realised that he too had heard me.

'*You must direct him,*' my Mentor said, '*for his landmarks have all gone. As he is standing he must go forward bearing slightly to his right.*' And so our sad little procession made its way, whilst I took instructions from my Mentor and relayed them to the grandfather and the boy, both of whom heard me. The women were far too concerned with the difficulties provided by their ailing children to hear my words. '*Stand close to him and we will transmit new strength through you.*' I put my arm about his shoulders as he stumbled weakly along. '*Tell him they can see the course of the river from here; it will encourage them. Ahead is the outline of its banks.*' Joyfully I transmitted this heartening news to them, and when they looked in that direction they began to feel all was not lost. At length my little party slipped and stumbled down the river's bank until they reached its welcome waters, where they refreshed themselves by drinking it, and then by washing as best they could. '*Now you must urge them to follow down the course of this stream for it will bring them eventually to human habitations.*'

I then addressed the old man called by the others 'Grandfather' although I do not believe he was any relation, but that chance had brought them together.

'You must follow in the direction this river flows,' I said to him. 'It will lead you to help.'

The old man looked wearily up from bathing his face, 'I have no strength to go on,' he began.

The boy broke in, 'Oh yes, Grandfather, we must do what he says. Look! He brought us here, didn't he? We should have died without water, you said so.'

One of the women who had been apportioning out meagre rations to the children, handed a small piece of food to him.

'Here, Grandfather, eat this, and we will go on. It is our only hope.'

And so once again I watched anxiously over my little party as they made their painful way along the banks of the stream. Occasionally I was instructed to give them a short cut where the river wound its way quite acutely one way or the other. The sun began to rise and they would stop more frequently for a drink, whilst the mother fed her baby which looked somewhat better than when I first saw it. '*They are gaining strength from your presence,*' I was told, '*but you must urge them on or they will not reach their destination.*' And this I continued to do. I really believe that every one of them was aware of my presence. One of the children even addressed a question to me.

'Where do you come from? You are not. . .' (and he mentioned a certain nationality). 'Your clothes are different.'

'He comes from God,' said the old man serenely, and with an air of finality. I felt deeply moved, and merely nodded my head in affirmation at the child, who appeared quite satisfied. It was a truly remarkable and wonderful experience to be able to make such close contact with my fellows alive on Earth, and to be able to help them so much more easily as a result. I found myself thanking God that I had been able to do so.

All this time there had been an improvement in the appearance of the country about us, gladly remarked on by my footsore travellers. It no longer looked dead and lifeless, for there was vegetation to be seen; trees had foliage and were no longer shattered stumps looking as though struck by lightning. At the same time this made their progress rather less easy, although it did mean that there were shady patches for them; also they found a little fruit on their way, of a sort quite strange to me.

It was around midday, when the sun approached its zenith, that my Mentor said, ' *There is a small village only two hundred yards ahead. Keep your party moving. If they delay it may be too late. The villagers are thinking of scattering for already they can hear gunfire.'* Once again I urged my party on, telling them that help was only a stone's throw away. How I longed to pick up and carry those poor little children whose strength had nearly gone. Indeed, they could scarcely whimper any more. ' *Go close to each one in turn,'* I was told, ' *and we will transmit power to them through you.'* This I did most gratefully, finishing with the boy who seemed least affected.

Suddenly, through a gap in the trees, there was to be seen a small dwelling, not much more than a hut.

'Look,' I said to the Grandfather, 'there is the village. Now you will receive help.' He let out a feeble cry and the others took it up, becoming quite excited, exhausted though they were. A dog barked, and figures began to emerge from the shade into the sunshine. When they were assured that here was no enemy but only a pitiful handful of refugees they hurried forward, and I was able to see my little band being given every kindness these poor villagers could afford.

As I stood beside them watching these ministrations, the old man turned to me, and bowing with a gesture of salutation he said, 'I thank you, sir, as I thank the Great Lord who sent you.'

I smiled at him, saying, 'May God go with you.' I do not think that the villagers heard or saw me, and the rest of the party were fully occupied. The children fell asleep almost at once, having first been given a little nourishment.

'You may leave. Your task is done. Close your eyes; there is more work for you.'

11

The Rescue of More Refugees

When I reopened my eyes I found myself in a small clearing
amongst the same type of trees I had just left. Here stood a few
small human habitations simply constructed of wood, bark and
dried leaves. Before I had time to take in any more my Mentor
spoke. '*This village has recently been under fire from opposing armies.
The inhabitants have all taken to the surrounding country for refuge. We
want them to know it is safe for them to return. You are to go into the
nearest hut on your right, and there you will find an old man dozing. He
expects to be killed by gunfire or bomb, but said he would rather this,
than continually drag himself into the jungle. Speak to him and tell him
the danger is past and he can summon his friends to return. The nearest
is not far off, tending his crops rather than wasting time lying idle. Go to
him now. He should hear you in his present half-conscious condition.*' I
walked quickly into the nearest hut, and saw, lying on a mat of
some fibrous material, an aged man, who appeared to be asleep.

'My friend, you need no longer fear death. The bombardment is over. Take courage, my friend. Rouse yourself and go to
summon the rest of your friends.'

'*Tell him that they will starve if they remain in the jungle, and that
his son-in-law works on the strip used last year for corn, this year for
tobacco*'

I passed on this message, and strangely it seemed to me that
this final piece of information roused him where the rest failed.
With an ejaculation he sat up exclaiming, 'Ah! That impulsive
young fool! Of what use is tobacco to us when we are in want!
He thinks he will sell it to foreigners for a good price.' I repeated
my instructions to him and he struggled to his feet. First he stood
in the centre of the clearing and called out as if to make sure
there was no one there. Then he looked into one or other of the
houses, and a few chickens ran about his feet as if hoping to be
fed.

'There is no one here,' I said, 'go and tell your son-in-law to fetch the others, for all is safe here now.' He turned as if he heard my voice but his eyes looked through me, and I felt a pang of regret to find that I was no longer in such close touch as upon my recent mission. Was that to be a unique occasion I thought sadly to myself?

'*Concentrate upon the work in hand,*' said my Mentor. '*These people may wander too far otherwise.*' I repeated my instructions to the old villager in peremptory tones, and saw to my satisfaction that he took hold of a stick and ambled off down a footpath worn amongst the undergrowth. I accompanied him, urging him forward from time to time for he was old and very frail. Before long we reached an open space off the track, a few yards to our right. Here was a crop of tall waving leaves, and in the distance I saw a man's head and shoulders as he bent over his work. My companion hailed him and he started up in some surprise and also, I felt, some apprehension, almost as though he feared he might be seeing an apparition. But when the old man spoke again, chiding him for what he termed his rashness in growing a crop so useless to the community, he knew that here was no ghost but his somewhat crochety old father-in-law, and ignoring the scolding advanced towards him, genuinely pleased to find him still alive.

'Ah, but the proceeds from this crop will purchase us those new tools we need.' Without waiting for an answer he went straight on, 'So you decided to take refuge after all?'

'Refuge! No indeed, the battle is over and it is safe for you all to return.'

Tell him to hurry up and fetch the others or they will starve.

But this stubborn old man was still grumbling about the crops, so I turned my attention to the younger one. 'He is right. It is safe now at the village. Go and call the others back, for they have little or nothing to eat with them, and you have provisions at the village.'

Without having given any sign of having heard me, he set his tools against a tree and set off through the jungle, announcing as he went that he must call the others to come home and that he knew where they were likely to be.

He shouted back over his shoulder, 'Go home and light us a fire, for we will be hungry.'

The old man turned, still mumbling to himself, and I was instructed to support him until he reached the safety of his village.

12

Supporting War Casualties

After this I was transported to what seemed to me to be another part of that same jungle, for the vegetation was much the same. I stood for the moment, feeling somewhat bewildered by the swift change of scene; then my Mentor spoke. '*There are two young soldiers here who have been shot down by their enemy. We want you to lead them to where they can be seen from the air by those who search for them. One of them is severely wounded and is suffering from loss of blood. He may be the one to hear you, as his hold on life is slender. Follow the instructions I give you.*'

I saw these two young men a few yards in front of me, seated at the foot of a tree. One had been bleeding profusely from the upper arm and the thigh. It seemed as though something had raked him all down the left side. His companion was attempting to adjust the dressing he had put on his friend. The wounded one lay back with his eyes closed, wincing with pain.

'You must make no delay in finding a clear space where your friends can see you. They won't see you here among the trees.'

To my surprise the wounded man opened his eyes and answered me.

'Yeah, that's right. It's no use our staying here. We must get clear of the trees. The search planes won't see a damn thing under these ruddy trees.' His companion looked at him in surprise but said nothing. 'You're right you know,' went on the first, 'we should find a clear space where they can see us. C'm on.' And he struggled painfully to his feet. 'What is it they always tell us?'

'Yeah,' answered the second, supporting his friend as best he could, 'but which way do you reckon we ought to go?'

'Bear to your left, where you see that tall tree shaped like an umbrella,' I said. 'Keep to your right of it, and then go down a slight slope.' I continued giving them instructions and at the same time I kept very close, especially to the wounded one so that power might be transmitted to him through me. It seemed to me that the wounded one was becoming weaker, nevertheless, and I asked if there was any other way in which I could help him.

'*Tell him to stop and have a drink, for he is dehydrated.*'

'Take a drink of water, my friends, for you need it to sustain you.' It became clear to me, then that he heard me for he at once asked his friend for the water bottle and they both took a short drink before going further.

'*Tell them to take heart, for they will soon be clear of the trees. One of your colleagues is attempting to direct the pilot of a low-flying aircraft over here.*' I passed on the good news, and the ailing one seemed to revive a little. Already the trees were thinning out overhead and the fit man commented on this, adding that his friend certainly had a genius for finding the way, though he phrased it in succinct colloquialism. No sooner had he spoken than they stepped clear of the trees and found themselves on a comparatively bare hillside. There was quite an extensive view over a shallow depression to more wooded hills in the far distance. '*Tell the wounded man to rest in the shade whilst his comrade finds a long branch to which he must attach something white to wave when the searchers come this way.*' I passed on this message and, faint though he was, the wounded man relayed it to his companion, who taking a knife out of his pocket soon cut a long sapling from a nearby grove and tied a piece of white stuff to it. It looked to me like one of the dressings from his pack. He gave his friend some more water and they both lay back exhausted, whilst I stood close by to lend them what strength I could. At length my Mentor spoke to me. '*The plane is approaching. In a minute they will hear it. Tell him to get well out into the open and wave his flag.*' I spoke in urgent tones, for the sick man was only semi-conscious.

'Listen! Your friends are drawing near. Move out into the open with your flag and wave it as a distress signal.'

Again it was the wounded man who responded to my words. He struggled painfully up on to his good elbow, exclaiming, 'They're coming! Get out into the open, quick.'

The other one said he couldn't hear anything, and anyway it might be the enemy.

'It isn't, it's ours.' The wounded man spoke with such assurance that his friend looked at him surprised. 'Quick, get out there quick. I can't.'

His friend scrambled to his feet and at that moment appeared to hear the welcome sound of the plane. 'You're right! he shouted. 'I know the sound of it.' Grabbing his long stick he rushed down the slope well clear of the trees and waited. Within seconds a low-flying plane appeared, setting its course along the shallow valley between the two banks of trees, its shadow undulating over the rough, scrubby territory beneath it. The soldier set to work frantically waving his improvised flag in wide arcs over his head, its extreme suppleness adding to the movement. He shouted, but the noise of the engines must have drowned his words. I prayed to the Almighty that they might be seen. Almost at once the plane began to alter its course, turning away from us and veering towards the belt of trees opposite. The soldier continued to wave; in fact, he redoubled his efforts, thinking he had not been seen. Suddenly it gave out a series of flashing lights, which I recognised to be signals. Great was the jubilation of the soldier. He stopped waving and translated the message for the benefit of his friend, who still lay back in a semi–conscious condition. '"We will return. Watch for survival chutes." They've seen us!' he shouted back over his shoulder, and then turned his attention to the flight of the plane. It circled and then came back, heading straight for the man on the hillside, releasing as it came two or three packages which then appeared to open flowerlike in the air, and float down to Earth to within a few yards of where the soldier stood. He, meantime, had been gesticulating towards his comrade as though to show them where he lay at the jungle's edge, at the same time clapping his hand on his arm and thigh to indicate whre he had been wounded, although by now they were climbing steeply in order to avoid the treetops and so were quite a height from him.

'*Go back to the wounded man. He is sinking into unconsciousness, and may not be able to take the nourishment dropped for them.*' I returned at once, and kneeling beside him put my hands on his brow as instructed. I remained here as long as I was told, praying as I did so, only dimly aware of the other man's activities retrieving and unpacking the neat parcels dropped for them. At length his cheerful voice broke in on my concentration.

'Here, drink this,' He held a small beaker. 'Someone had the right idea, they sent us three kits, so we got three of everything.'

He supported his friend whilst he drank a few sips at a time. After that he tried to persuade him to eat something, but he was too weak to take more than a morsel or two, so his friend set to work to prepare a little soup, and this he managed to swallow. The wounded man then fell into a light sleep whilst his comrade watched him anxiously, meantime taking some nourishment himself. I stood keeping watch over my two charges and praying that help might come in time for the sick man. I then heard the voice of my Mentor. '*Help is coming. We want you to warn them, so that the able man is ready to make their presence known.*'

'Help is on its way.' I said. 'Prepare yourself to signal to them where you are.' The fit man made no reaction to my words, but continued to eat and drink.

I spoke more sharply.

'Your rescuers arecoming. You must be ready to signal your position or they will not see you.' This time the wounded man awoke, and attempting to sit up groaned with pain.

'Take it easy,' said his friend, hurrying to his side, 'You just lie there, pal. They'll be coming soon.' I knew he was saying this to encourage the wounded one and not because he had heard my words.

'They're coming now,' gasped his friend. 'Get your flag ready. They can't see us here.' And he fell back again.

Still unbelieving, but obviously remembering the accuracy of his friend's former predictions he looked round for his wand.

'Hurry up.' I ordered, 'and get down the slope into the sunlight.' This time he may have heard me, for he said good-humouredly that he'd got the reception party ready. He was starting to amble downhill when he suddenly heard the distant sound of an engine, and his movements quickened into almost hysterical action as he leapt down the hill brandishing his little white banner and shouting, 'You're right. God, you're right. You must have second sight or something.'

A strange object came into sight, quite unlike the bird–like machine which had flown over earlier in the day. This came more slowly and seemed to make more noise, as for one thing it was closer to us. It seemed to hover like an ungainly dragonfly before choosing where it might settle. Then slowly it subsided on to a more level patch of ground below my friends. As soon as the circling blades above it slowed down a door opened and two men hurried down, some steps to the ground. They were dressed in somewhat the same clothing as my two soldiers, but wore distinctive arm bands. I stood still beside the sick man, whose life seemed to me at a very low ebb, whilst his friend hurried up to the team of rescuers. I saw him point urgently up the slope. In no time they all three returned to him, holding a stretcher between them and a pack of medical equipment which they proceeded to use with utmost skill and dexterity.

'*They are determining his blood group from certain records on him. There is nothing more for you to do. His Guides will support him now.*' As I was told this, one of the men looked up asking, 'Where's the other man? We were told there were three of you.'

My cheerful friend looked up in astonishment. 'Three? No, only two of us. The others had had it. How we got out I'll never know.'

'We were told three,' said the medical attendant laconically, without looking up, 'one in white. Thought it sounded funny.'

'Well that's all right. We got three rations dropped!'

'*The observer was a sensitive and saw you,*' my Mentor told me. '*Close your eyes. You have done well.*'

'Will he recover?' I asked anxiously.

'*It is doubtful. He has lost too much blood. Everything possible is being done.*'

I felt myself being transported in the usual way. Opening my eyes I found myself in my Guardian's shady garden, standing underneath a tree, and there approaching me down the path was my dear Guardian himself. He smiled at me and I became aware of the soothing peace his presence brought, in contrast with the menace and the tension experienced in my latest missions.

'Oh, my Master!' I exclaimed, 'how terrible it is to witness the ills men inflict upon one another.'

For answer he took me by the hand, and leading me towards his pool of cleansing waters he said, 'Immerse yourself, my child, for though you have had no direct encounter with the evil ones who oppose God's will, you have been contending with the results of their wicked actions, and these coarser vibrations will have contaminated you. I shall wait here for you.' So saying he seated himself at the head of the pool, whilst I stepped gratefully down into its refreshing water. This time I did not swim

vigorously as before but merely lay contemplating the trees and
sky above me, and the scenes I had so recently witnessed passed
rapidly across my mind. With them came a sense of shame, for I
too had fought my fellow men and more than once must have
inflicted just such injuries as those I had seen: the wounded, the
homeless refugees and a desecration of the very land itself.

At last I could bear it no more. Leaving the pool I hurried to
my Master's side. Falling on my knees in front of him I cried,
'Oh, my Master, forgive me, but I find myself unfitted for this
work, for I too have inflicted pain and injury in battle upon my
fellows when I fought for my King in this very incarnation in
which I have chosen to manifest.' I paused and looked anxiously
into his face to await his response to my words.

For a few minutes he looked at me very seriously and then he
said, 'It is for this very reason that you have been sent into an
area of conflict, for in this way you are not only helping present
day mortals, but you are making amends for having harmed
God's children in another age. Under certain circumstances it is
sometimes inevitable that man should find himself obliged to
oppose his fellows by all the physical means within his power.
For even though such measures are totally against the will of
God, nevertheless, the ways of man have become so far
removed from His ways that there are occasions when the forces
of evil must be met on their own ground or they would hold
mankind within their grip for evermore, causing him eventually
to destroy himself and all about him. This has happened before
within the universe, we are told. Until man has learnt to conduct
his life according to the will of God there will continue to be
occasions when force must be met with force, and here it should
always be remembered that the true motive for the use of this
force must always be borne in mind. The action may degenerate
into that of the evil ones, should anger, hatred or vindictiveness
be allowed to gain the upper hand, or indeed any base motive
whatsoever.'

He paused, and I stood up eagerly asking him, 'Then you
believe that I am fit to continue my training?'

'It is not for me, nor for you, my child, to determine whether
or not you are fit for this undertaking. You would not have been
chosen as a candidate were it not considered by the highest
authority that you were suitable, in fact by The Great One
Himself.'

Impetuously I took hold of his hands, saying, 'Oh, how clear you make everything appear to me. At one moment I felt myself to be quite unworthy of this work, and now you have made me see things in quite a different light and I feel reassured. Thank you, o my Master!' I dropped his hands and stood before him, waiting to hear what he would say.

He looked up at me smiling benignly. 'Sit here, my child, for I have something of importance to tell you.'

I sat beside him and waited for what it was he had to say.

'Far from being found unworthy of being an aspirant for The Company of White Knights, you have been judged worthy of being promoted to becoming a full member of the illustrious Company whose members seek only to serve God.'

My elation was such that for the moment I felt myself quite unable to reply. I had never even dared to look forward to this happy day, regarding it merely as a far distant point in time which I might eventually be fortunate enough to reach. At length I managed to utter a few disjointed phrases of joy and of gratitude to the Master Tetheera for his share in my initial training, and finally asked whether I might continue to seek his advice and to benefit from his wisdom and healing presence, for I found the prospect of having to do without his help quite daunting.

'Indeed you may continue to apply to me for help, my child, and I will be happy to give it, for I feel that our relationship, rooted in the long distant past, has blossomed once again. Now I must tell you that the Ceremony of Initiation will take place shortly, but before that you are to attend a service of dedication in the Temple, or as you might prefer to call it, coming from your era, Chapel, which belongs to The Company of the White Knights and stands within their Citadel. Come with me for I am to present you.'

So saying he led the way up the garden path and into his spacious room. There he left me for a moment while he went to a recess with doors across it, which were carved in a most splendid and yet restrained manner, here and there glinting with inlaid gold and the bone of some animal. From it he took some elaborate and, as I adjudged, ritualistic garments: a head–dress which resembled a bishop's mitre, and a carved wand about the length of a forearm, which he held in his left hand. He approached me and taking me by the left hand led me along the cloisters in the opposite direction to my usual way, and we found ourselves entering the Knights' Chapel. This was unlike any building I have ever seen before, for to begin with its walls appeared to me to be translucent, as though made of some exquisitely fine marble or alabaster, through which a bright sun was shining. My Guardian, however, did not permit me to stop and admir, it but continued on his stately way, leading me up a flight of shallow steps which also appeared to have a light of their own within them, and into an inner sanctuary of smaller proportions. Here the light was more subdued but still seemed to emanate from the very building itself. The light in the main body of the church, which was about the size of a small cathedral, was a soft white, which nevertheless glowed with a certain indescribable warmth; but in the inner Temple, or the Sanctuary, it was of a faint bluish tinge, becoming here and there almost a violet.

I took my place beside my Guardian amongst the other novices, and found they were standing in a circular formation. As we stood there others came in and joined us, until there were about a hundred of us. I closed my eyes to the scene about us, wishing to concentrate my thoughts in prayer to God that I might prove worthy of this great honour being accorded me.

13

The Service of Dedication

As I stood praying silently, within my mind I became aware of a wonderful sensation of love which seemed to envelop me and keep me fast within it. This was a sensation I never remember having experienced before, and I can assure you I will never forget it. My whole being appeared to be one with this entirely benign and loving presence; I also felt at one with the entire universe, and as though there were no such thing as hatred and evil within it. I longed to remain in this state of ecstasy for ever, but I felt that it was gradually waning.

'Oh, do not leave me!' I cried out within my mind, for I felt sure that this presence was none other than God Himself.

Then I heard, again it seemed within my mind, in loving tones of reassurance, 'I am always close beside you, for you are one of my own darling children.'

Astonished I opened my eyes to see whether any of the other Initiates had heard these words, and I saw on every face a look of rapt attention, as though each were listening to some inner voice. At the same time I observed a most beautiful shaft of light which seemed to come through the Temple ceiling and focus itself upon the ground in the centre of our circle. We stood for some time in this enraptured state, only aware of the marvellous peace and love which seemed to draw us all together as though united into a whole, and yet retaining our individualities. Suddenly I knew what it was to be a child of God, for I became aware of His infinite love for us in spite of our many imperfections and transgressions from His law. I felt myself to be utterly secure in His love, and I knew that had I been a most hardened criminal yet would He still continue to love me. As I was made aware of this remarkable, almost overwhelming, truth, I heard a voice speaking warmly yet gently to us. It seemed to emanate from the shaft of light which fell before us, and I had no doubt whatsoever in my mind that it was the voice of God Himself.

'My beloved children, I wish to thank you all for the services you have accorded me already, whilst you carried out your work of training before becoming initiated into The Company of White Knights, who have served me through long ages in the support of my dear children, who must manifest on Earth in order to gain the experience they require for their souls' evolution. Their mortal bodies, due to Satanaku's disobedience to my word, operate upon a heavier vibration, therefore, than was my will, rendering them vulnerable to all the ills and accidents which befall the frail mortal body which he in his arrogance evolved for them. Their spirits too were set at risk for this same reason, since they are for the most part unable to hear my word and act upon it. Indeed it was for this very reason alone that he created their physical bodies in such gross matter that they might not hear my will, but must hear him or his evil counsellors (as did he in the first place, when he was tempted into gaining dominion over those spirits whom I sent to manifest on Earth). Bitterly he regrets it now, but the law of freewill operates throughout the universe, and even I could not prevent him from carrying out his wicked plan. As a result of this act of disobedience on the part of Satanaku (whom I had put in charge of my little planet Earth, or Terra), the forces of evil, who oppose my will throughout the universe, were enabled to influence man from the very outset. In this way they led him astray from my ways, thereby bringing about the sorrows which have afflicted him ever since and which were entirely contrary to my will; for I would not have one single child of mine suffer in any way at all. To have had to watch generations of them suffer, as they have done, from his very first act of disobedience, has grieved me more than you can ever know or understand. I tell you this, my children, for it has a bearing on the work you are about to undertake, and upon the work you have so successfully undertaken already; for you will witness at first hand the way in which the forces of evil can bring about the destruction of man in many devious ways, and how they will even assault my animal kingdom. Indeed, the very planet itself has also been set at risk. Not only through wanton misuse of its surface and surrounding atmosphere, but also through the introduction of that great force known to man as nuclear power, long before he was mature enough to be entrusted with it. You, my dear children, will be sent on missions the nature of which will be varied, and I do not expect you always to be successful, for your opponents have at their command immensely powerful forces hitherto unrecognised by man, although he has witnessed the results of these forces from time to time when large scale disasters have been attributed to natural causes. I can assure you that the majority of these disasters have been brought about by the manipulation of electric forces of a lower speed than was ever intended to be used on this small planet, and although I foresaw the outcome of these manoeuvres, nevertheless, with the forces at my command I was frequently unable to counteract them.

'The reason for this, my dear children, is that, in order to counteract these forces used by the powers of darkness, I must deploy my own in such a way as will ensure that no harm will come to my own children. For although they are discarnate for the most part –' and here He lowered His voice to even more loving tones than before, so that I felt my heart would melt within me, '– I am fortunate in having the services of a few of my incarnate ones who come to work for me whilst their bodies lie sleeping on Earth, yet they are still vulnerable to these heavier rays. Were I to allow them to encounter the full force of these heavier vibrations of a lower wavelength than that on which you, my children, exist, they might find themselves quite numbed by the onslaught and even unable to cry to me for help.

'You must understand, my children, that without a request from you for help I am unable to render it as effectually as I might were you to link your minds with mine, for there will be no electric current flowing between us by means of which I am able to direct those forces which can come to your assistance. I want you to take particular notice of this, so that if ever you find yourselves in difficulties, or in danger of being overpowered by the forces who oppose you, you will remember to call on me, for I shall come instantly to your aid. Never leave it so late that you are scarcely in control of your senses, for in this state they may even hypnotise you into obeying their will, and it could mean many an age before you can be rescued from their thrall. Another warning I would give you is: never to answer their taunts, however tempted you may be to do so, for if you do you will provide an electric link with them just as does your cry for help with me. Now, my dear children, I shall give you my blessing. Step forward one, by one to kneel within the circle of light. I am very pleased to see so many of my children qualified to become members of The Company of White Knights.'

So, one by one, we stepped forward and knelt within the beam of light, taking our turns as indicated by our Guardians. When my turn came, following that of the Initiate on my right, I stepped forward, my feelings a strange mixture of pride and humility. Pride that I had succeeded in qualifying to become an Initiate, and humility before the presence of Almighty God, whose greatness and whose love permeated the entire building. As I knelt I closed my eyes, turning my attention inwards. A wonderful feeling of peace came over me, and I heard a voice within my inmost mind say, 'Well done my trusted servant. I have watched all your valiant attempts to help your fellow men now imprisoned in mortal bodies on Earth, and I have rejoiced at your successes and grieved with you in your losses. Know that I am ever close beside you, darling child, and do not take risks by not calling on my name when you are hard pressed. Go, and my blessings go with you.'

At this pronouncement I felt a sudden warmth flow through me, and murmuring within my mind, 'I thank you, o Almighty God,' I stood up and withdrew to my place, whereupon the Initiate on my left stepped forward. I felt myself to be greatly encouraged by the promise that God Himself would be always close at hand, and I resolved to remember all His advice, for in this way I should avoid all danger. The thought of falling victim had not even occurred to me, and I shuddered inwardly; the thought of becoming a slave to them, and of being obliged to carry out their evil plans, filled me with dread. Why had I not been warned? I had supposed that novices would not be sent into situations of such danger, but I now saw that it might be possible.

When every one of us had received his or her blessing and had returned to his or her original places, I became aware of the most beautiful music coming from some invisible source, beginning very softly as though not to intrude too suddenly on our thoughts, and then gradually rising to a triumphant climax. At last our Guardians led us away, one by one, as we had come, and I walked back with the Master Tetheera in a dazed condition, the music still ringing in my ears. He directed me into his garden, and I paced about its exotic glades and its well-ordered precincts, trying to control my tumultuous thoughts. At last I saw my Master approaching me. He had taken off his ceremonial robes and appeared to me a more familiar figure.

'My child,' he said, 'very soon you must attend the Initiation Ceremony in The Great Hall; but first, are there any questions you wish to ask me?'

I stood still for a moment not quite knowing where to begin. At last I managed to say, 'Oh, my Master, I am still living under the influence of the wonderful ceremony which I found so moving and so deeply inspiring that I find myself quite unable to formulate any questions. There is one, however, that I feel I must ask you, and that is, may I still turn to you for advice and support, after I have been initiated?'

'You may indeed, my child, and I shall be happy to give you all the help that I am able, when you enter upon this new phase in your career.'

I felt a great sense of relief when the Master Tetheera said this, and, springing up from the bench on which we had seated ourselves, I stood before him and bowing according to the custom of my era I thanked him in most heartfelt terms. Finally he said that I had become very dear to him, as though I were his own son, and then he said it was time for us to go to the Great Hall for the Initiation Ceremony.

14

The Initiation Ceremony

We walked along the cloisterlike corridor to the Hall and on our way we saw many other initiates all going in the same direction, the newly created ones being accompanied by their Guardians. I felt myself to be supremely happy and not a little proud, I must confess. When we reached the Hall my Master directed me to my place in the front amongst the other new initiates, but not before he had pointed out to me several friends and relations of mine, who stood amongst the spectators and who smiled loving encouragement to me. My grandparents I saw were there from that life I had spent in France, and some comrades at arms. There were also with them others whose faces were somehow familiar and yet I could not identify them, and I learned later that they had been very close to me in yet other lifetimes, which made it more difficult for me to recognise them in my personality as Jacques Delacourt. I found myself standing between a tall African of splendid physique whose ebony skin was enhanced by his white tunic, whilst on my other side stood a lady whose origins were I should say from the Far East. In fact I learned afterwards that she came from the island of Formosa. Her appearance was that of small, neat proportion reminding one of a figurine such as is seen in china cabinets, although of course she wore the tunic of The White Knights. I exchanged smiles with my two neighbours, and then looked about me. In front of us, on either side, stood rank upon rank of those Knights who were already fully initiated, with here and there a gap left for us to fill. Amongst them I saw my Uncle and other companions waiting to receive me, and I felt myself to be almost overwhelmed with pride and joy.

Throughout these preliminary arrangements there was to be heard the most beautiful music which seemed to come from a

gallery above our heads, with choirs singing either unaccom-
panied or to the accompaniment of orchestras, and sometimes a
great organ filled the Hall with sound. Suddenly, however, it
died away, and I saw a brilliant shaft of light before us in the
centre and just in front of the ranks of Knights; there within the
light I recognised the beloved figure of Jesus, our Leader. His
smile seemed to encompass us all and I felt his great love for us
emanating from it. Then he spoke.

'My dearest ones,I have watched your valiant struggles
against the enemies of God, our Heavenly Father, and now you
are to be enrolled into the ranks of The Company of White
Knights no longer as novices but through your own merits as
Knights yourselves, and I know now that I can count on each
and every one of you to carry out the task assigned to the very
utmost of your ability. In this way we shall be able to continue
the fight against the powers of darkness, whilst at the same time
helping our brothers and sisters who are incarnate on Earth, and
who for the most part are unable to hear the words of God
speaking into their hearts. Nor can they hear His Holy
messengers or guides when they seek to advise or instruct in the
ways of God. For until the time comes when Earth's vibrations
may be speeded up, and with it the speed at which God's
children operate, only those few who have been trained through
many lifetimes to hear the voice of God, those who desire to
continue on the path of evolution, or have some debt they owe
society or who wish to help mankind in his harsh lot, will return
to Earth, only to find themselves at the mercy of the evil ones
(whose words are easier to hear, since they operate on the same
low vibration as Earth conditions.) It is to guard them against
listening to these vile insinuations and suggestions which may
be fed into their minds by what is generally termed telepathy,
that we work.

And here I must warn you to be ever on your guard
yourselves, for there is nothing the evil ones would like better
than to lead one of my own true Knights astray because he had
listened to their words, thinking them to be those of his Mentor
telling him what to do next. Only pray to God at all times and
you will never run into this danger, for your mind will be
operating on a higher wavelength than that of the evil ones, who
are not able, by their very nature, to rise above a certain speed.
Should any one of you, however, feel himself to be tempted

beyond what he feels is his capability to resist, he should immediately ask that he be removed from the scene and that someone take his place. My dear ones, do not be ashamed to take this step, for it is braver by far to admit our failings than to fall into the trap set by the cunning wiles of an implacable and totally destructive force pitted against us. I would not have one of you fall into any harm, for you are very dear to me.'

After that, he went on to say that besides protecting our fellows incarnate on Earth from the suggestions put to them by the evil ones, we would find ourselves sent to help those who were in some physical danger, again very often engineered by the evil ones in the first place, although in some instances it could also be due to the foolhardy action of the person or persons in question. Added to this were those dangers commonly described as 'acts of God', although in reality he said they were no such thing, for He would never deliberately harm His beloved children. Rather, they again were almost invariably a direct result of the manipulation of the electric forces at the disposal of the evil ones who work constantly to harm man; although in some cases seemingly natural disasters are in fact due to man's own foolish or selfish behaviour. In carrying out this work of rescue, whether we were fighting the elements or whether we were attempting to save man from something made of his own design, such as a vehicle of some sort, we were to remember that, in times of crisis, incarnates' subconscious selves can the more easily transmit messages through to their conscious selves, so that we should never give up the attempt to transmit vital instructions to them. He also reminded us that when we felt ourselves to be really hard pressed we were to remember that we should call on his name and he would always come to our assistance. He concluded up by saying:

'And now, my beloved ones, I pass on to you the blessings of our Heavenly Father, whose love knows no bounds.'

At this, we were directed by those who acted as stewards throughout the ceremony to advance one by one and kneel before our great Leader, who then placed his hands lovingly upon our heads, and as we rose to our feet placed the insignia of The Company of White Knights on our breasts. This is in the form of a gold cross within a circlet of gold. We were then led to our places to fill the gaps in the ranks of the Knights who stood waiting for us. I found myself to be beside my Uncle, whose noble face shone with pride, and I felt my pleasure to be complete. Throughout this part of the ceremony could be heard the most beautiful music, though never so obtrusive as to distract one from the ceremony itself. Finally, when we were all in our places, and whilst some glorious chords were played on the organ, Jesus, our Leader, gradually faded from sight as he was transported to another plane.

My Uncle and I then made our way to our friends within the congregation, and together we strolled about the spacious grounds belonging to our Citadel. I received many congratulations and compliments, and also enquiries as to the nature of my missions. Before long, however, the assembled company began to disperse, as one by one the Knights were summoned to go out again on some mission, and when our turn came we bade our friends goodbye and hurried back to the Great Hall. I knew that as an Initiated Knight my tasks would be of a more demanding and a more testing nature.

PART

2

*An Initiated
Knight*

1

Preventing the Spread of Nuclear Technology

On opening my eyes I saw that we were standing in a large building, which I am told that you call a factory. I was told at once to go and stand by a doorway on my right. There was no door, as it was merely a gap between one set of machinery and another. No sooner had I stationed myself here than I saw the body of a man lying motionless at my feet. I thought for the moment that he was dead, but then he moved and attempted to sit up.

'*Tell him he must sound the alarm. It is of the utmost urgency.*'

'My friend, you must take courage and rouse yourself to sound the alarm. Come, I will help you. It is of the utmost urgency.' And I stood close to him praying that strength might be given him through my proximity as I had learnt was possible. To my surprise he did indeed begin to rouse himself, although I could see the poor fellow was making a supreme effort.

'*Hurry him,*' said my Mentor, '*for his attackers will return any minute. Not only will they kill him, but they are endeavouring to take with them vital information which is highly dangerous in the hands of malefactors.*'

'Hurry, my friend, or you will be too late. I am helping you.'

The wounded man, for I could see he had had a severe blow on the back of his head, staggered uncertainly to the wall between the two chambers and propping himself against it he reached up a hand, as though unable to see properly, and fumbled with a small box–like structure on the wall, at what should have been about shoulder level. His fingers seemed to have no strength and were beginning to lose sense of purpose.

'Be quick, or they will come back. I am helping all I can but you must sound the alarm.'

As though in response he renewed his attempts, and then I

saw he must first open a little door, as it were a small cupboard. It was evident that the poor man was scarcely conscious.

'Hurry, my friend, you are doing so well.'

Again he responded to my words and this time his fingers obeyed his mind, and as the door opened he felt inside and seemed to press something inside with a downward motion. Instantly there was a loud clamour seeming to come from every direction, of a high-pitched, incessantly repeated note.

'Well done, my friend!' I cried, delighted with his success.

'*Tell him to hide behind a bench immediately.*'

Alas, my poor friend had expended all his strength on his brave action to sound the alarm, and to my dismay he slithered to the floor and lay inert. Nothing I could say would rouse him. An instant later some men came rushing through the chamber in which I had first found myself. They wore masks of some thin material stretched over their heads and slippers on their feet which would make no noise.

'Here's the ––––––– who did it!' yelled one above the noise of the alarm.

'Thought you'd killed him, did you? Well, let's make sure of it this time.'

To my horror he fired several shots into the body of my hero. A great anger swept through me.

'*Control your emotion,*' said the calm voice of my Mentor, '*for it is wholly negative and will allow entry to the evil ones.*' With an effort I mastered my feelings, at the same time feeling myself to be this man's murderer, although indirectly.

Almost at once I was transferred to another scene. This time I found myself at a warehouse, evidently a part of the same concern as the working area I had just left, for here too were masked men ransacking the place in what appeared to me to be a frenzy.

'*They are searching for a vital piece of equipment which will tell those for whom they work all they wish to know. They know they have not long, for the police will already be on their way. We want you to direct their attention away from the far right hand corner from where you stand.*'

I advanced to the nearest man to me, saying in my most military voice, 'Go at once to those shelves beside the door.'

To my surprise he responded at once, and turned to the area to the right of the door.

'Call your comrades,' I said, and again he reacted.

'Here! We forgot to look here.'

Two men came to join him, and I saw some of my colleagues shadowing them. I also saw to my dismay, that there were some of our opponents drawn from the forces of evil, who were overshadowing the men at the further end of the warehouse.

I reported this to my Mentor, who said, 'We know, but you may go there and support your colleagues.'

I hurried to the further end and took my stand beside the Knight already there, who turned out to be the newcomer from South America.

'My friend,' I said to him, 'let us call upon Almighty God for help to vanquish these evil ones.'

He nodded, and silently we both prayed for help. The effect was instantaneous and took even me by surprise. A shaft of brilliant light fell before us as we stood confronting those menacing figures. They gave a shriek and fell back in disorder.

'Go,' I said, 'go whence you came, and leave God's children in peace to obey His will and not your wicked master's.'

I spoke with some vehemence, for the memory of the murdered man was still in my mind. At any rate they fled I know not where, with wild unearthly shrieks. Thanking God I turned my attention to the searching men.

'Come, you are wasting your time. The police will be here any minute. Leave while you can. You must give up and run for your lives.'

One responded and with an oath said, 'Come on, it's no good. They'll get us if we don't go. Quick!' He ran out, but two remained and I and my friend addressed each one.

'Leave it,' I said to my man as he persistently grabbed down package after package and prised open boxes. It was evident that he was a very determined man.

'Your friends have all left,' I said. 'If you find it you will not manage it yourself.' This last was purely guesswork, for I had no idea of the size of the object for which he was looking. In any case, he did not seem to hear me.

'*Tell him a murder has been committed,*' said my Mentor.

'One of you has committed a murder here. You had better clear off before you are accused of it.' At last I seemed to be reaching him, and he paused uncertainly. 'They killed the man who set off the alarm. Get out quickly.'

He stopped altogether, and looked up and round him like a hunted beast.

'The fools,' he muttered, and followed this with a string of oaths.

'Get out, I say. Can't you hear the police!'

With a furious movement he flung away the metallic object he had been examining and rushed to the nearest door. On seeing their ringleader bolt, the other followed as fast as he could. My eyes met those of my colleague's and he thanked me for my help.

'*Your work is finished here*,' said the voice of my Mentor. '*stand together and we will transport you*'

On arrival we were sent to the cleansing waters in the grounds, before our next mission, after encountering the evil ones. Reassembling in the Citadel we found most of the others already there, and were able to confer amongst ourselves before once again we found that we were being despatched to a new scene.

2

Helping at an Avalanche

This was of a very different nature, for we found ourselves in a picturesque setting which appeared to be a little village set amongst the mountains, although I could not at first make up my mind where they were, but judged it most probably to be Switzerland, though I had never visited it in my last life. We stood together, a small group of discarnate beings in the middle of a bustling community of incarnate men and women, who went their way quite unaware of our presence.

'*You have been sent here*', said my Mentor, '*because there is danger of this entire village being engulfed by an avalanche of snow and rocks, and we want you to warn the people. Reports are coming in of heavy falls of snow above here, but they are not being taken seriously enough. We want you all to go to anyone in a position of authority and to impress on his mind the urgency of the situation. You are to go first to the Pastor. His house is beside the church and he has just arrived home for his midday meal. Go at once.*' I saw before me a quaint little church with a belfry surmounted by a small steeple. I hurried to the house beside it and made my way inside. There I saw the Pastor removing his warm outer clothing and shaking off the snow before hanging them up. He called to his wife, whose voice greeted him from another room. He opened the door on his right and went across to a large central stove where he made some adjustments. Then he looked about him.

'The children should be home from school by now. I hope they are not playing around.'

His wife came in from another entrance, carrying a tray with steaming dishes on it, which she set down on the long table. Then greeting her husband with a kiss she answered, 'I have sent them for the night to stay with the Traubers. There were warnings of danger in this area of the heavy snowfall causing an avalanche. I could not reach you and it was the last bus to make the journey today, so I felt I must act quickly.'

The clergyman looked somewhat surprised, but he said after a little thought 'I believe you acted very wisely, my dear. I myself have felt uneasy, but I missed the latest forecast as I was on my way back at that time.'

'*Speak to him now,*' said my Mentor.

'You are right to be uneasy, there is great danger for this village,' I said, standing close beside him.

His wife continued with further explanations so that his mind was occupied, but during a silence between them I spoke. 'There is great danger here, Pastor, and it is your duty to warn the people of this village.'

No sooner had I spoken to him than his wife reacted to my words, whilst he appeared not to have heard them.

'Oh, Martin! I feel we should all go to safety. . . everyone here. I feel sure there is great danger.'

'Madame, you are right,' I interposed. 'Your husband should make it his duty to warn everyone to give them a chance to escape.'

I feared for the moment that she too remained unaware of my words, and I repeated them even more vehemently. I believe now that I was mistaken and that she had indeed heard me and was pondering on their implications, believing them to be her own thoughts.

'Martin,' and she spoke with such urgency that her husband instantly fixed his eyes on her face, at the same time registering surprise. 'How would you set about warning the whole village?'

'Why, my dear, they all hear the forecast on the radio, just as you and I do. There cannot be a soul here who has not access to a set of one sort or another.'

'That is not enough,' I interposed again. 'They do not understand how grave is the danger.'

To my surprise the lady repeated what I had said almost word for word. 'That is not enough. They must be made to realise the danger.' She looked at him intently.

'My dear', said the Pastor, 'how can you be so sure? You look quite strange and unlike yourself.'

'Oh, Martin! You know very well what can happen. It has happened before in these parts.'

'My dear, I will telephone and arrange for you to join th

children if you are so worried.'

'It is not for myself alone that I fear, but for everyone. And do you think for a moment that I would go without you?' Her eyes flashed for a moment at his inability to comprehend her meaning. 'Finish your meal. I am going to the schoolhouse to consult with Mlle Souzaine. I found her most sympathetic with my fears this morning, for she said she wished that all the children could be moved to a safer district.'

Gathering up some dishes she retreated to the kitchen, removed and hung up her apron and then passing through another door found herself in the hall and proceeded to muffle herself in her outdoor clothes.

'*She hears you, believing it to be her own thoughts,*' said my Mentor. '*Tell her to advise her husband to go to the mayor and urge him to arrange a total evacuation of the village.*'

I did so, and once again she repeated my words almost verbatim. Pulling on her gloves after she had tied a scarf under her chin, she said, 'Why don't you consult with M. le Mayor? He can arrange transport for us while it I still light.'

With that she left the house and I saw her figure, bent against the blowing snow, hurry along the street, for I had been told to remain with the Pastor. Hurriedly the poor man gulped down the rest of his meal and drank his coffee; I could tell his mind was in a turmoil, for he was unable to make up his mind as to his best course of action, and had not the advantage of hearing my words as had his wife.

'*Speak to him again*', urged my Mentor.

'My friend, you must move fast, for the danger increases hourly. Hurry, hurry, or you will be too late.'

I do not know whether he heard me or not, for at that moment the telephone bell rang and he hurried to answer it. The instrument lay on his desk and he sat down reaching across to it.

'*Stay close beside him and continue to impress his mind. It is the Burgomaster or Mayor himself who speaks.*'

'Yes, yes, Bernard.' Then he paused to listen. 'It is true that Hélène has sent our children down to our relatives for fear of avalanches. She acted on her own initiative following on the bulletin on the weather, for I was out of reach. And now she is at the schoolhouse in order to urge a close down and to persuade the parents to do the same as we have. Mlle Souzaine is in complete agreement. Why do you ask? You have received official warnings? Certainly I will do all within my power if you just tell me. Is the road still clear? . . . Ah! They have sent help up. May I suggest that you give me a list of those not on the telephone and I will go round advising them of the facilities you have arranged for their immediate departure, whilst you telephone the rest? Alphonse can ring the church bell, and if you issue him with instructions he can then pass them on. First I must notify my wife.'

Agreement was reached on all points and my Mentor told me that my task there was done.

When I reopened my eyes I found myself on what seemed to me to be an endless expanse of snow which lay at a steep angle beneath my feet, and I certainly would not have been able to stand where I was had I been in mortal frame, but in our dimension I found myself to be quite impervious to Earth's gravity.

'*Exert your powers of concentration,*' I was told, '*for through you we are directing the necessary electrical force to maintain this weight of ice and snow in its present position long enough for the people in the village to escape. Most of your friends are here engaged on the same work.*' I noticed them then, placed at intervals along the steep mountain slope, their figures appearing to me almost luminous as they stood motionless and as though wrapped in thought. '*Allow yourself to become quiescent. Nothing more is required of you. You are merely the means by which we direct the current into the area where it is needed. On the other hand the forces of evil are doing their utmost to dislodge the great load of snow that it may engulf all life below it, by means of their slower vibrations.*'

And so I stood quiescent, trying to empty my mind of all thought, that I might become the better instrument for God's will, dimly aware of the whirling snowflakes and the white mountainside. It seemed timeless, as though I had slipped into eternity. Then I became aware of a most unpleasant sensation, almost as though my whole being were being shaken to the inmost core, and I began to feel my senses grow numb. At the same time everything about me seemed to grow darker. Can this be the avalanche beginning to move, I thought, but at the same moment dismissed the idea, for I realised it could not affect me.

'*You are being overshadowed by an evil presence*', said my Mentor, and his voice sounded distorted and far away. '*Pray for help.*' The word 'pray' somehow penetrated my dimming consciousness and I clung to it. 'Pray, pray,' I thought.

'Please help me God,' I managed to say within my mind, and instantly those dreadful sensations I had been experiencing stopped and I regained my senses. An unearthly shriek sounded in my ears and I found the darkness had gone from me, and I was left again standing on the gleaming snow. Swiftly I offered up a prayer to God for saving His child; I dare not think what might have become of me had I surrendered to the all but paralysing sensation which had come over me.

' *You are particularly vulnerable when you render yourself quiescent without having first prayed for protection.'* I thought to myself that I would never again allow such a thing to happen, and I there and then prayed to the Almighty for protection. Immediately I felt secure, and a warmth of love seemed to flow through my being.

Following this alarming experience and the subsequent sense of the protection I was being given, I resumed my vigil on the mountainside, noticing that already it was beginning to grow dark, and before long we seemed to be in total darkness, though I was scarcely aware of my companions. The snow itself seemed to give off a certain luminosity and I found myself wondering how long it would remain in position. My Mentor chided me for allowing my concentration to relax, and once again I relinquished myself to the power which was being directed through me.

All at once I became aware of a sudden movement on the surface which lay before my eyes. It moved slowly, then gained a terrible momentum whilst at the same time there was a great roaring sound like a giant wave of the sea, and this was accompanied by the sharp sound of cracking as though there were immense whips being brandished in the air.

'Close your eyes. There will be rescue work to be done. Some refused to leave their homes.'

I did as I was told and on reopening them found myself on the edge of what appeared to be a precipice, for there was nothing but darkness below the sharp white edge on which I stood. I experienced a moment of fear, as though I were still in mortal frame.

'You are on the roof of a farmhouse which is all but engulfed by the mass of snow and stones which have descended. We want you to direct your concentration upon the mountainside above it. If no more descends and these people remain where they are, they stand a chance of survival.

Below them lies a ravine and certain death, for their house has been moved bodily. Help will come eventually.'

Once more I stood quiescent, allowing myself to be the conductor for the necessary electrical force which was being directed by those highly evolved spirits in charge of this operation; but this time I made sure that first I sent a prayer to God that I might be protected from the forces of evil who are forever on the look-out for unguarded moments in the lives of His children. I saw two of my colleagues stationed a little way from me, one to the right and the other to the left.

Again I lost all sense of the passage of time until I heard my Mentor speak. *'We want you to join the rescuers and pass on our instructions. One of your colleagues is taking your place here. Close your eyes.'*

The next moment I found myself close to a party of six men who were having to fight for every step they took up the steep track which had been obliterated in many places. However, at least one of their number was familiar with the terrain, and the expertise of the leaders was remarkable. I felt I knew why I had been sent, for the men spoke French, my native tongue as Jacques, although the accent and intonation were somewhat different. Although a different language in itself provides no problems to us on our missions, yet nevertheless one's own language creates a certain affinity which again I believe to be a matter of electrical vibrations.

They were now close enough for them to see the perilous position of the farmhouse, for they had powerful lamps, added to which the morning sky was just beginning to lighten. They debated, as they climbed, the chances of anyone's being alive.

'Tell them yes, three are alive, but they must hurry for they are very cold and becoming exhausted.'

'Hurry, my friends. Three people are alive in there, but they need help quickly.'

Whether or not they heard I don't know, but one man quoted a similar case where survivors had been found.

'Be quick, or you will be too late,' I said in my most peremptory tones.

'In that case we must hurry, or they will be frozen to death,' said one, but I think he was answering his friend not myself.

'Tell them to approach with great caution and from this side, not above. They must tunnel a way to the side of the house.'

I gave these instructions to the man who was leading the party. He had paused and appeared to be sizing up the situation.

'We must be very careful,' he said, 'the balance is obviously liable to be precarious. As I cannot assess conditions on the mountain at the back of the house, it would be best to break our way through the wall. In fact, it is almost inevitable.'

'I believe there to be a door and also a window on this side,' spoke up another.

'As the situation is, my friend,' said the leader, 'that is immaterial, for speed is of the utmost importance. At the same time we must move with extreme caution, in order not to risk dislodging the mass above us.' So saying he began to work very much in accordance with the instructions I had passed on to them.

Place yourself above the working party and we will try to contain the pressures from above through you and your colleagues.'

I did exactly as I was told, for, remember, in my dimension I require no foothold, being supported entirely by the electrical forces of the wavelength on which I operate, or, should I say, exist. Once again I resumed my timeless vigil, unaware of what was taking place below me, until I was told that the rescuers had completed their work and had managed to bring out two survivors; the third, being elderly, was already dead. I was told to accompany the party down the treacherous pathway and to lend strength particularly to those who bore the stretchers. Fortunately they had not far to go. My sad little cortège wound its way down the slope until it halted in a flat open space where some of the snow had been cleared, and there were other rescuers at work shovelling it by hand, and also using mechanical equipment. It suddenly came to me that we were standing in what had been the centre of the village, but which had now become a shapeless mass of churned up snow, soil, boulders and uprooted trees. The only building which was at all recognisable was the local hostelry, and this appeared to be the centre of activity. My party made its way towards it. Had the Pastor and his wife escaped? I found myself wondering.

'There is more work for you here, I was told. *'Two rescuers are themselves trapped. Two of your colleagues are supporting them. We want you to impress the organiser to send help to them. He stands by the inn door. Say to him: "Tomas and Jacques have been gone a long time".'*

I obeyed my orders immediately, and had the satisfaction of

seeing this man look up sharply, saying, 'Tomas and Jacques have been too long. We must send someone at once to follow them up.'

Three men volunteered.

'They went to check up whether there was anyone in that house opposite the church,' he told them.

The church itself was no longer visible, and the debris lay thick on the ground. Fortunately these men appeared to have no doubt as to the location of the house they were to search. To me it appeared as another snowdrift. They followed some tracks round to one side, and here someone had worked with a shovel until a splintered door was exposed, the steps up to it still hidden. One of my party forced his way in sideways, shining a lamp into the dark interior.

Almost at once low groans could be heard, and the man who had pushed his way inside gave a sharp exclamation. 'Quick! Bring an axe and we shall need some lifting gear. There is a man trapped here. Hold on . . . help is coming. Do not attempt to move.' Outside he said, 'We shall need some of the medical staff. The poor man must be in pain.'

'*Tell him there are two men in there,*' said my Mentor.

I repeated this to the rescuers.

'Don't forget, both Tomas and Jacques are reported missing,' said one, and the first man forced his way in again followed closely by two more and myself, albeit unknown to them. The weight of the snow must have telescoped the top part of the house into the ground floor, and when the would-be rescuers had forced their way in they had probably dislodged some precariously placed beam which then fell with all that was above it on to these men.

'Only Tomas lives. Jacques was killed instantly. It is the dead man they see. They must seek further for the other.'

I passed on this information.

'*The owner of the house was trying to make his escape when he heard the noise approaching, and he is in the store-house at the back, best approached from the outside. He is alive but very cold. Hurry them.*'

The team were dealing very efficiently with the injured man, and so I spoke to a man outside who appeared to be overseeing the operation. 'The owner of this house is trapped in his own store–house and requires immediate help. You must approach it from the outside for safety.'

My words seemed to bear fruit, for he said, 'Can you identify that man?'

'Yes', replied a local, 'we've found Tomas. Jacques, poor fellow, looks pretty bad. In fact I do not think he can be alive.'

'Then where is the owner of this house? A shop, wasn't it? I was told he refused to be evacuated.'

'That's right, he wouldn't go.'

'He is in the store-room at the back,' I repeated vehemently. 'You must work round to the back outside the house. It is too dangerous inside.'

'Maybe he's in his store,' said the local man, 'counting it up.'

'Ay, plenty for him to eat in there.'

'And drink,' put in another.

'Call them to order,' I said peremptorily. 'This man's life is at stake.'

Again the supervisor appeared to hear me. 'Here, you and you, come at once and show me the outside approach to this store. No time must be lost.'

Obediently they led the way, and it became obvious that a great deal of snow and debris must be shifted. The operation was entered into with every available man helping. Once the injured man was safely out of the danger of the shop, and the corpse of his unfortunate companion removed, they were able to move with less caution. A mechanical digger was brought into action which pushed the snow and soil aside; it also had an automatic grabbing device which proved of immense use.

A cry went up when at last the outer door was revealed. Surprisingly it remained intact. As the door was found to be very securely locked, the foreman of the rescuers ordered that it be left as it was for fear that in breaking it down a further displacement of the wreckage might take place. It required a less vigorous attack merely to smash the little window to one side of the door, and a man squeezed himself through it.

'Tell him the shop owner is on his right. He managed to scramble on to an empty shelf and to pull up some sacks to keep himself warm.'

'There is no one here,' shouted the rescuer, 'it's just a mass of wreckage and goods thrown about.'

'There *is* someone here,' I urged him. 'Look to your right. The shelves have supported the debris and he is there.'

'Hold on! called the rescuer. 'He might be over here', and he pushed his way with utmost caution, bent double as he did so, towards the shelves, some of which could be seen by the light of his lamp.

'You are perfectly right,' I said. 'Examine the shelves.'

The man let out a cry as he fumbled about in front of him.

'He's here! He's alive but unconscious. Quick, someone give me a hand to get him out.'

'Unlock the door,' he was told. 'It is in a precarious state, and we will try to hold it up for the rescue operation.'

I stood in the centre of this little tumbledown store with its jumble of spilled groceries and splintered beams at an acute angle, and remained still and remote from the human activity about me.

Finally I was told that it was finished and that the shop owner had been extricated more dead than alive.

'But he stands a chance. Your friend the Pastor has escaped too, as he and the mayor and their respective wives had escorted the final party down the mountain. Only a handful of obstinate inhabitants remained; some have paid with their lives. The rest have been rescued and will be removed for there is continued danger. You may return to the Citadel.'

As soon as we found ourselves back in our beautiful gardens we went at once into the cleansing waters, for we had all been subjected to the lower vibrations of the forces of evil, and these must now be neutralised by the waters especially prepared for this purpose at God's command. After that we were told that we might take some time off to ourselves until we were summoned to go on another mission. My first thought was that I should visit my grandparents and report to them all my astonishing experiences; but before that I must visit my Master Tetheera and tell him about the terrible experience I had had on the mountainside, for I wished to hear a fuller explanation than I had been given, or rather, than I had been able to have in the heat of battle, as it were. I found him as usual at his studies, but he set these aside, as soon as I ventured into his apartment, and advancing greeted me warmly.

'Sit down, my child. You have come to ask my advice, I believe.'

I suppose there was a certain look on my face, for I had said nothing; but I then described exactly what had occurred, saying that it had left an indelible memory on my mind, and that I had felt myself to have been in grave danger of falling completely into their power.

'It is true,' he answered, 'that indeed you might have done so, for evidently you were not sufficiently protected by prayer on this occasion; but, since fortunately you had hold of your senses enough to survive this terrible experience it may prove to be of inestimable value, since the shock you received will serve to remind you never to leave yourself unguarded again.'

'Certainly it will serve to do that!' I exclaimed. 'But at the same time there are one or two points I should like to bring up with you, my Master. Firstly, is it not true that we are protected at all times?'

'Indeed you are sustained by God the Great One who makes possible the very continuance of your existence upon whatever plane you are manifesting; but at the same time a direct request for help from you to Him provides that link necessary for His electric forces to be sent to you, which not only protect you but make it possible for your Guides and Mentors to make the necessary contact to issue their instructions.'

'That answers my next question in part,' I said, 'but not wholly. Upon arrival at a new scene for another mission I invariably pray for protection from God, and also that I may be successful in carrying out His work, so why then was I not sufficiently protected on this occasion?'

'My child, it is not surprising that you should feel a certain disappointment at the discovery that you were still open to attack from the opposing forces, even though you had already petitioned God for protection. I myself am to blame in that I did not foresee this contingency during your training as a novice, and for this I must ask your pardon. But the fact of the matter is that when you render yourself as a quiescent channel through which power is to be directed for some specific purpose, you are extremely vulnerable, for your thoughts are turned inwards upon the object of your concentration, and you are no longer aware of what is taking place in your immediate vicinity. Though I confess to be at fault for not having warned you beforehand, I must in fairness point out that a newly initiated Knight is seldom appointed to so dangerous a task at such an early stage in his career. It indicates the urgency of the situation and also that your Mentors considered you to be worthy of this assignment.'

'There have been other occasions, o my Master, when I have been told to render myself quiescent in order that I might be used as a channel for the powers my Mentors were directing for some specific purpose. Perhaps through good fortune I have escaped harm.'

'If by good fortune you mean luck, my child, I must tell you that there is no such thing, for I must remind you of the law of cause and effect. In these past instances I can only assume that your prayers were sufficient to protect you, or what is more likely still that you were not in direct opposition to the forces of evil, but were sent to deal with the results of their works, so that none of their entities were present.'

I reflected on his words, reviewing certain of my missions and reached the conclusion that he was perfectly right. I said that I believed that that was indeed the cuse, and he then proceeded to expatiate on the subject.

'When the forces of evil have succeeded in setting in motion certain events calculated to cause distress and even injury to human beings, as for example engineering a fire in a home or place of work, they may retreat and leave it to take its course, in which case those of God's servants who are sent to help in rescue operations will not encounter the evil entities responsible. Where, however, they are sent to prevent the disaster from actually taking place, there they are far more likely to confront the enemy. Sometimes it will be found on investigation that the causes for any one disaster lay in the past, perhaps even centuries ago in earth–time, but that recognition of the inherent dangers in a certain set of conditions had been carefully masked from men's minds, so that only a very far-sighted person, or one who could hear the warnings given from this plane of existence, would become aware of the risks ahead. They may be physical, or of an altogether different nature, such as a lowering of moral standards, or the exploitation of people who are not in a position to protest, or the loss of their livelihoods, or persecution of an intolerable nature. In all these examples the seeds had already been sown which would eventually bring trouble to mankind. Nevertheless, you are not to know this when you arrive at the scene of your mission, so you should make a rule of praying for protection at once. Moreover, should you find yourself in direct opposition to one or more of these entities who serve a master other than God, you should pray for special protection, mentioning the fact that you find yourself in contact with them. Again, where you are requested to render yourself quiescent, as you were on this occasion, you should explain the circumstances, before putting yourself into that vulnerable state. As a result of your request a special guard will be put on you until such time as the danger is past. Afterwards it is fitting that you should render thanks to the Great One for the protection He has granted you.'

I thanked the Master Tetheera for his explanations and advice, and bowing I made my farewells, and went to visit my grandparents, having first informed them by telepathy that I intended doing so.

We met again at our old home, which by the way, appeared as though it had been just newly built, and with none of the signs of weathering to which I had become accustomed when I was on Earth. Indeed, in some respects I was not sure that I liked it so well, for it seemed to my eyes to have lost some of its character. But this may have been because I had spent so many happy years in it as it had appeared in my day. My grandparents advanced to meet me as I approached the steps before the main entrance, and they embraced me warmly, saying how proud they were to have not only a son but a grandson now serving in the ranks of The Company of White Knights.

I felt very proud and happy myself, as we paced about the old precincts and I described to them some of the situations in which I had found myself, the action which had been taken and the outcome of them. They were immensely interested and moreover they made several pertinent comments and suggestions, which were to prove useful to me when I remembered them at a later stage. I began to see what a large part their influence had played in the forming of my character in that life, and felt that now was the time to thank them. Accordingly I expressed my thanks, somewhat to their surprise; but they appeared to be most gratifyingly impressed by my accounts and professed to be proud of me. This filled me with joy and completed my happiness.

'You were always a good boy,' said my Grandmother, patting my hand, 'and we expected much of you.'

I caught my Grandfather's eye and knew he was thinking of the same incident as I myself.

'The trout pond!' I exclaimed.

'Ah!' cried my Grandmother. 'He disobeyed you then, I grant you. But I said at the time you were merely tempting the boy by forbidding it to him.'

I looked at my Grandmother in some surprise. 'But Grand-mère, Grandmère, I thought you feared for my life?'

'No indeed, I knew you were a strong swimmer or I should have kept watch myself. No, your Grandfather thought you would frighten away his precious fish down the stream, and he dearly liked trout for his supper.' She smiled indulgently at both of us.

'No, I was not a good boy then; but I remember being severely punished. You said it was a dangerous pool, and I had set a bad example to the younger ones!' I expostulated.

'A boy was reputed to have drowned there, long before our time,' answered my Grandmother. We continued chatting and reminiscing until I was summoned to join my fellows again.

As soon as we had arrived at our new destination I could tell that this was to be another rescue operation.

3

A Flood

Although it was night somewhere on Earth, there was to be seen a swirling mass of water which appeared to swallow all within its pathway.

'It is a flood of terrible proportions,' my Mentor explained. *'you are to attempt to save human life. On your right is a man who clings to a treetrunk. Tell him his son holds on a few yards away and needs his help or he will let go.'*

I at once identified these victims of the flood, and spoke to the man in vehement tones. 'Your son is nearby, but he needs your help or he will drown.'

At once he responded by calling out the boy's name, which sounded to me something like 'Pete'. At any rate the boy gave a choking somewhat feeble reply, but evidently it was enough for the man to hear, for he worked his way through the mass of branches and debris until he was able to assist the boy to reach a more secure position. 'Thanks, Dad,' I heard him say, 'I couldn't have held on much longer.'

'I know,' said his father, and I felt him to be surprised at his own words.

'Well done!, said my Mentor. *'We are now putting you on a rooftop where a family has taken refuge. You are to see that they remain there and not venture off it before help comes.'*

At once I found myself astride a wooden housetop a few feet above the water, which seemed to race past on either side. I myself had no need to hold on, but I could see the difficulty of the poor little family at my feet, for the roof was wet and slippery and afforded little support. They sat round the hatch, which was open, so that they gained some purchase by hanging their legs down inside the house itself, and indeed two small children sat on the top steps of the stairway, which looked to me of a more temporary nature than a normal staircase.

'Tell them it will soon be light, when help will come,' said my Mentor. *'At all costs they must not attempt to move or they will be swept away.'*

I passed on this message, but was unsure if anyone heard me. They remained huddled together, the five of them, obviously suffering from shock.

'The man is worrying as to whether the house will stand. Tell him it will.'

I passed on the message.

This time the wife said, 'Oh well, I am so thankful the house is strongly built. It will stand up to this, I feel sure.'

He looked at her wonderingly, although she could not see him and did not answer.

'She is quite right,' I put in, 'it will withstand the flood.'

'Who's that man behind you, Mummy?' asked one of the small children, a little girl sitting on the top step.

'There's no man here, dear, just us,' her mother answered, but I felt a great sense of relief that one of them could hear me.

'Yes there is,' said the child. 'I heard him say the house would be all right.'

'Someone's voice carried here by the wind,' said the father.

'It wasn't.' The child spoke with assurance. 'It was quite close. He made me feel good inside.'

'Oh, Sally Ann, you're such a fanciful little thing!' murmured her mother.

Very soon it began to get light, but this seemed only to add to their distress, for they could now see the extent of the devastation around them, and they commented on the loss of various landmarks in tones of horror.

'Help will soon come,' I assured them, praying for its appearance with all my heart.

When the daylight increased we at last heard the sounds of human activity. Boats were seen approaching and low-flying aircraft plied their way across the sky backwards and forwards. At one point the father sprang up, gesticulating wildly to a passing aircraft, but nearly lost his balance in so doing. Both I and his wife told him to keep still, and she brought out a white handkerchief to wave. Soon a rescue launch made its way towards them, and they were hailed by loud–speaker from it and told to remain where they were. I had the satisfaction of seeing rescue operations of great competence getting under way before I was recalled, my mission completed.

4

Change of Heart in a Scientist

Our next mission was of a very different nature, for we were sent to a research laboratory.

Here our Mentors told us, *'Your opponent, are attempting to instil into the minds of the men who experiment, new and horrific ways of decimating the human population on Earth, should war break out between major powers. You are to post yourselves close beside any worker whom you see in danger of being impressed by one of the evil ones.'*

I looked round and saw at once a youngish man bending over his bench, whilst leaning directly over him almost as if whispering into his ear was a dark, grotesque figure, whom I recognised instantly to be one of our opponents. I approached it at once, praying as I did so for protection, for I could experience the sensation of a much lower vibration emanating from it than that upon which we ourselves operated, and an unpleasant dizzy feeling came over.

I reported this at once to my Mentor.

'Stay where you are and concentrate on the human being, and we will see that you are protected,' I was told, and almost at once a feeling of relief came over me, as the opponent's electrical field was neutralized. With a snarl it turned on me, and then vanished, I cannot say how nor where.

I stepped close to the young scientist, praying that his work might be wholly in accordance with God's will, and for the benefit of mankind and not its destruction.

'Stay with him,' instructed my Mentor. *'He came to Earth to carry out important work in the field of medicine and came to this sphere for purely economic reasons, and at the instigation of the evil ones who saw in him a useful tool for their own ends.'*

I stationed myself close beside this man, and bent my will on him. He sighed, somewhat despairingly, and with an impatient

119

gesture pushed his work away from him. I found myself pitying his dilemma.

'Do not relax your attention,' I was told. *'Continue to impress him with his rightful mission.'*

I moved even closer to him, and found myself bending over his shoulder as had that sinister figur before me.

'Do not waste your gifts on this wholly destructive work, but rather use them as God intended for the benefit of mankind.'

The result was startling in the extreme, not only to myself but to the human occupants of the room. He sprang up with a cry and rushed out, brushing past anyone who came in his way.

'Follow him, and strengthen his resolve. He is one of their key men, and they will not let him go easily.'

So I accompanied this poor man through all his subsequent interviews, in order to maintain his strength of purpose. I was even sent home with him when he had to confront his family with the startling intelligence that he had given up his present work,, nd intended going over to medical research as he had originally planned. This would entail a lowering of all their living standards, as they immediately recognised; but fortunately his wife was sufficiently fond of her husband to set his interests and well-being first. Moreover, when I spoke to her, putting his case clearly before her, she appeared to hear me, judging by her response.

Finally I was withdrawn from the scene, and rejoined my colleagues in the Great Hall of the Citadel, where we were able to compare notes on our various experiences. I shuddered inwardly when I heard what some of them had discovered about the evil work being undertaken by this state-supported laboratory, and I prayed fervently that it might be closed down altogether. It was while we were conversing that we were told to assemble together in readiness for our next mission.

5

Influencing a Town Council

For this we were sent to a meeting of Councillors, in what appeared to be a town which had once flourished on account of its industrial undertakings but which, we were told, had been overtaken by changing demands and techniques, rendering their industry, once so prosperous, now a decaying one. The attendant financial issues were now being laid before the Town Council.

There were present those who genuinely concerned themselves with the welfare of those people whom they represented, but there were also a few who set their own interests before all else, my Mentor said; and these men were being influenced by the forces of evil, who had no need to send their dark entities to impress them, for they had already established links with them and could speak directly into their minds, as would modern man through a telephone.

'We will tell you whom you are to support and whom you are to oppose,' I was instructed; but in fact it soon became apparent, as the arguments proceeded.

At the moment they were discussing the need for a new football ground for the use of the young men of the city whose aimless lives were forever leading them into trouble. The opponents of the scheme declared that it would only be destroyed; 'vandalised', was the word they used; whereupon the scheme's supporters said that full-time organisers and coaches must be employed. The others answered, that there were no funds available for such an enterprise, and, moreover, it would yield no profit.

'Then we must continue to repair damages done by idle youngsters, and where's the profit in that?' put forward one man.

121

'What proof have you that such a project would end vandalism?' sneered his opponent.

'These projects have proved invaluable in other places,' replied another Councillor, bringing out a sheaf of papers.

'It doesn't follow it would succeed here. They're a tough lot, remember.' He looked 'a tough lot' himself was my impression, and he went on to put forward alternative proposals, which in the main seemed to be new shops with adjacent car parks on the area under discussion. The objections raised to this were that existing shops already lacked sufficient custom, and the owners would certainly raise objections.

'Then let us demolish them,' came the reply, stunning most of the Councillors by the sheer ruthlessness of the proposal; and I knew instinctively that the proposer intended to benefit from his own proposition, and cared nothing at all for the interests of others. The conflict continued for some time, whilst I and my colleagues threw our weight into the scales as best we might. Eventually the meeting was adjourned, but several negative, if not wholly bad, proposals had been prevented from being passed. Our Mentors withdrew us, saying that we, or another group, would attend the next session.

6

A Dying Man

On our arrival back we were sent almost immediately on another mission, this time to a sick man's bedside, where it became apparent, and indeed we were warned, that certain members of his family were trying to persuade him to leave his fortune in a manner altogether different from the way in which he had disposed of it in his Will. The poor man, already weak, was being further weakened by the vehemence and total lack of consideration for his feelings, and his medical attendants were in despair, but found themselves quite outnumbered.

'You are support this old man in his last hours,' I was told. *'He has made a fair Will, and should be left in peace. There is nothing to be said for his persecutors.'*

I stationed myself close to the patient and spoke reassuringly to him, whilst my colleagues attached themselves to the ones who so callously disregarded his real needs. Very soon a look of peace came over his face, and I felt that my reassurance had not been in vain; besides which, as he grew weaker, I felt he actually became aware of my presence, for he opened his eyes and appeared to look at me, saying, 'You are right. I have done what I thought best for everyone concerned. I thought it all out a long time ago, long before I fell ill.'

'Then you are right to stand by your decision,' I answered.

He smiled and closed his eyes again, thanking me telepathically. His persecutors withdrew, some shamefacedly, and some unrepentant and with indignation, and at last the sick-room was quiet, to the infinite relief of his attendants. We too were withdrawn from the scene.

'He will be cared for now by his own spiritual Guides and Mentors,' we were told.

123

So ended one of the shortest and the most distasteful missions on which I had been sent.

Before being sent on another mission, I was told by my Mentor to go to my Guardian once more. I hurried to his apartment, wondering what was in store for me. He greeted me with great warmth of feeling and ascribed to me my usual seat, the lion stool on which I had sat so often.

7

The Origins of the World

'My child,' he began, 'you are to receive some instruction on the origin of the Solar System and its place within the Universe. Certain other of my pupils are to attend my class as well, by the command of the Great One.'

I knew by now that this was the Master's manner of referring to God. I also noticed that a semi-circle of chairs and stools had been arranged facing his carved chair, and that behind him were suspended various diagrams which I took to be the maps of the celestial spheres, as indeed they turned out to be. Before long my fellow pupils arrived, six of them, and one, a Chinese lady, from my own group. We greeted each other warmly, for we had fellow feelings arising from our many shared experiences. The Master Tetheera then addressed us, first with words of welcome, and then telling us that God Himself had ordained that we receive this instruction on the origins of the Solar System in which we were manifesting.

The Solar System came about in the first place because God, or the Great One, ordained that it should. Putting it in simple terminology for our benefit, he said that God set aside, or willed that a mass of certain gases should be directed into this part of the Universe formed from the galaxy to which we belong. He has, to carry out His orders, certain entities who are well acquainted with this work, having been trained to do it by other great spirits, who in turn had learnt it from others. Their duty is to direct electrical forces, supplied them by God, in order to provide the motivating force for the manipulation of the gases ordained to become a new planetary system. In the first place the whole mass was concentrated into one unit, and this unit was then compressed by the forces at their command until it could no longer contain itself but burst forth into many long streamers

125

which shot, of their own volition, out at different angles and at different speeds, each exactly as ordained by God, who issued forth His instructions and formulae into the consciousnesses of His faithful servants, who obeyed His every order. These streamers formed themselves into globe–like masses, each turning on itself and thus providing its own source of gravity. Each of these globes, however far distant from the original mass which we will now call the sun (for that was what this new star was destined to be), finds itself answering to the pull of that largest of all bodies in the system, the sun itself. He went on to say that the chemical composition of the different incandescent globes of gas now encircling the sun, varied and were laid down exactly by God as He desired them to be. Moreover, He also ordained the speed at which they should turn or revolve on their axes, and the number of moons, or satellites, they should acquire from the surrounding space. In all this, we were told, the hand of God was to be seen, and no mere chance happening ever occurred; nor did any one event grow out of another of its own volition, as your present day scientists would have us believe, he added sardonically, for every circumstance which arose during the creation of our Solar System had been ordained and supervised by God Himself.

Having said this, he then went on to explain that the only factor which had to be taken into consideration was that of the Force of Evil, which operated throughout the entire Universe and which opposed God's will at every opportunity. This force, he went on to say, is of a wholly destructive nature, and bears no allegiance to God, whose ways it appears to detest. It too operates by means of certain electrical powers, the origin of which no man knows, but what is known is that they are of a heavier, slower vibration than those used by God and those who serve Him.

When a new Solar System is formed, and this event we were given to understand is by no means so rare an occurrence as might be supposed by man, the Forces of Evil show themselves to be particularly anxious to be present at the outset, for it is their aim to implant within these newly forming heavenly bodies their own electrical forces; by this means are they able to influence its future life. Moreover, should this body be destined to support life in any shape or form, they are thereby enabling themselves to take control; and, in the case of man, to lead him as far from the ways of God as possible, ultimately causing not only his destruction, but very likely, the planet on which he was living. Once they have directed their rays into the substance of any planet they will have the power to control its future, and only an arduous campaign undertaken by especially trained and dedicated servants of God can rid the planet of the bonds which bind it to the evil ones, who will fight with desperation and yet with infinite subtlety to maintain their hold on their prey.

The Master paused here and surveyed our upturned faces. 'Ah!' he said. 'I can see by your expressions that you have all grasped the significance of my words. Yes, our own planet Earth fell a victim to these evil ones, and has suffered for it ever since. Go, my children. I shall expound this, next time.'

This he did, by telling us that the vulnerable time in the life of a planet was whilst it was still molten and in the process of cooling down. This was when those set in charge should be most on their guard against the onslaught of the evil ones. In the case of Earth, an Archangel named Satanaku had been set in charge by God. He was insufficiently prepared for the force of the malignant rays which were directed on him by the enemy, so that he became, as it were, numbed by them, and later acquiesced to the demands made upon him. Had he but recognised the jarring notes of this unfamiliar force as being out of harmony with God's own electrical forces, he might have sent out a cry for help in the form of a brief prayer.

Tetheera said, he need only have said: 'Please help me, Father, for I am being assaulted', when immediate help would have come; but that although God Himself was fully aware of what was happening He might not act, on account of the universal law of freewill which He must observe as well as His children. Therefore He had to watch not only His Archangel, but also His newly forming planet Earth, fall into the hands of the evil ones. More than one attempt was made to prevent the subsequent sufferings of man by the sending to Earth of highly evolved spirits who had only to request of God that man be removed from the scene altogether, since the planet had been rendered unfit for him, and it would have been arranged by God that this should happen. But these messengers of His, great though they were, became themselves incapable of hearing God once they were incarnating in the heavier vibrational forms which Satan had evolved for man under the direction of the evil ones, and so their requests became of a more prosaic nature and they requested such things as food and shelter for sorely pressed early man. These God supplied by various methods, which Tetheera said he would describe to us later in the course. But the outcome for Earth was inevitable, he said, from the moment Satanaku submitted to those false electrical currents directed on him. That is to say: infinite suffering, privation, and in every respect the contrary to God's will, must be endured by His beloved children destined to manifest on this planet. To begin with, he said, God had not intended us to live in bodies of such gross material that they were subject to every ill known to mortal man, and prone to accident by nature of their frailty; for living in these bodies, which operate on a slower wavelength than that which was ordained, meant that we were unable to hear the word of God spoken into our minds. This in turn meant that we could not lead our earthly lives according to God's wishes but in our own wilful ways, and in so doing we have brought on ourselves all the ills of this world.

The role of man as ordained by God was to have been to nurture and sustain the lowliest forms of life. These He would have sent to Earth by means too advanced for our comprehension, and then as time passed and these species became more highly evolved, we were to nurture that vegetation which would be required by these different forms of life. Man himself would have been operating on a higher wavelength than the fauna and flora sent to Earth, so that his physical self would have been scarcely visible to our mortal eyes, and he would have been sustained entirely by the electrical rays directed on him by God. Man himself would have been directing the appropriate rays on to the different forms of life on this planet. Had this come about, man would not have suffered the terrible physical ailments which have been his lot from the beginning, and which God, his sorrowing parent, has been obliged to witness.

He then explained the manner in which it came about that we mortals had been made to manifest in bodies other than those designed for us by God. This was entirely due to the defection of Satan who, having himself fallen prey to the forces of evil, was now in their power and listened to all they had to say, and obeyed their commands. They persuaded him, easily enough, that if he caused man to manifest in bodies of a denser texture he himself would then hold dominion over man, who could no longer distinguish the words of God, and would therefore obey only Satan. This idea of holding dominion over all the souls who came to Earth delighted Satan, who was then told how to carry out his plan.

Firstly, he must persuade the female entity who had been sent to him to carry out God's wishes on Earth, (she who has now come to be known as Eve), to allow her own vibrations to be lowered so that her physical self became more substantial, and operated at a lower speed. He then required her to cohabit with a species of ape which the evil ones had caused to be introduced to Earth together with that form of vegetation it needed. Eve rebelled against him on both counts, recognising that he was disobeying God's will. As a result Satanaku became furious with her, and finally she appealed to God for help; for, although she had been sent to serve under this mighty Archangel, nevertheless she was sufficiently evolved to be able to form her own judgement, and she realised that Satan was behaving in an uncharacteristic way and in defiance of God's instructions. Moreover, the idea of mating with a beast of a lowlier order was totally abhorrent to her, and she refused. Having requested help and having revealed Satan's plans (although, in fact, God was fully aware of them, but needed a direct request before He could act) she received it at once, in the form of another great spirit, known to us as Adam. His role was to protect Eve from the wrath of Satan, who when he found she had reported his designs to God reviled her even more than before, and out of revenge, at the instigation of the evil ones, evolved for the human race a form of reproduction so painful and so hazardous that it proved to be fatal in many cases. In fact, its hazards have only diminished in very recent times. Not only did he do this, to revenge himself on all spirits manifesting in female form, but he also spread about the entirely false story that it was Eve who had disobeyed God, knowing full well that he himself was the culprit. Eventually, his version of the story came to be incorporated in the Jewish Scriptures as we now know them on Earth, although it bears no relation to the truth. Had Eve succumbed to his will and carried out his evil intents, there is no doubt that a race of being would have resulted, hideous in form; and, what would have been worse, without that sustaining link which God desires to have with all His children. This can be provided by prayer nowadays, but in those early days on Earth would have been by direct speech into their minds. Not only would this uncouth species have been unable to interpret His word, but the spirits dwelling within them would have been of an altogether lower order, and they would have been further removed from the Divinity of God. This divinity would have dwindled with each succeeding generation; as it was, Adam and Eve's progeny, (through no fault of their own but purely because the force of evil had caused Earth's wavelength to be lowered), manifested in the more substantial bodies desired by Satan, were in part led astray. Certain of them cohabited with an ape-like species of the animal kingdom, thereby producing offspring owing little allegiance to God. This delighted Satan, until he found that he too had little control over them, for they answered to their true masters, the evil ones. Before long they took to destroying one another, and so began Earth's long, sad tale of the cruelties of war.

In answer to our unspoken question, Tetheera said,

'Set your minds at rest, my children; this unfortunate species has long since died out, and none of their descendants now exist on Earth, for the forces of evil will always cause their servants to be self-destructive, nor are they able to create anything that is good and worth preserving.'

He then told us that early man had found himself presented with so many problems in his daily struggle to survive at all, in the harsh surroundings in which he found himself, that the human race nearly came to an end at a very early stage in its history, but that it had been saved by those highly evolved spirits, who sent up prayers to God for help, and as a result God caused certain edible crops to be transported to Earth; for example, wheat, and various fruits. Then primitive man was instructed by those same highly evolved beings, or 'old souls' who had experience of many other lives in other parts of the Universe, as to how to cultivate his crops, and to construct shelters to protect him from the elements. These 'old souls' had volunteered to incarnate on Earth for the express purpose of helping the younger ones who were inexperienced in the art of surviving under so many difficulties, and they were sent to communities most in need. Their undoubted capabilities were recognised whilst they were still at an early age; they came to be revered almost as god-like beings; and, long afterwards, they were referred to as very patterns for their fellowmen, until they became tribal legends handed down from generation to generation. In this way they founded the mythology of that country. It must be understood that these volunteers from earlier epochs were able to hear and to interpret the word of God and to pass on His loving advice to His children.

He then went on to tell us that mankind would continue to suffer all the ills of this world until it had learned to live by God's true laws and precepts. These have been brought to us at intervals in our history by those great spirits who volunteered to act as His messengers. These messengers incarnated, or appeared as mortal man, where and when God decided the location and the moment to be propitious; they recognised before they came that for the most part they would meet with opposition from all those whose interest it is to maintain the old order, and from the great mass of humanity, to whom change of any sort represents an element of uncertainty, which generates a sense of insecurity which they are unable to tolerate. And so these brave souls returned to Earth fully aware that they risked persecution or even death if they held to their resolve to overthrow the old regime and its beliefs. In all cases God ordained that His messengers should incarnate under circumstances that were most favourable for His law, and caused them to be born at the same time as those spirits in the immediate environment best able to act out supporting roles to His chosen messengers. One grave error commonly made by humanity, he said, was to mistake these splendid messengers of God for divine beings, and to come to regard them as God Himself come to Earth. In point of fact they are no more divine than are we all, for we are all children of God and have within us that spark of divinity which He, God, gave us at our first creation. This misconception is always encouraged by the forces of evil, who will lose no chance of denigrating God or His Holy Ones, and they will then do all within their power to bring His messenger to some ignoble or untimely end. He cited as an example our great Leader, Jesus, whom, he said, God had never intended to suffer the cruelty and ignominy which he had had to endure; but rather intended that he should have continued to teach as he had begun, together with his cousin John and their disciples in all the lands round the Mediterranean.

Nevertheless, he said, in this instance the evil ones over-reached themselves, for it was this very act of cruelty which caught at the attention of the populace. Succeeding generations came to believe that he had suffered on their behalf, so that they came to revere this act of attonement, as they saw it, and to love and admire him who had made it, instead of deriding him and his followers, as had been intended by the forces of evil.

Seeing the looks of astonishment on the faces of those of us brought up as Christians, Tetheera paused, saying that he realised how this must strike some of us as heresy. Nevertheless, he went on, we must at all times be prepared to accept the truth when presented with it, if we regarded the source as being reliable. Here he smiled, saying he trusted he came into that category.

He then proceeded to tell us how the forces of evil had gained complete mastery over yet another planet within our Solar System, that which had orbited next to the giant Jupiter, but which is now represented merely by fragments of rock which continue to orbit along the selfsame path as a once beautiful planet known in heavenly circles as Uranus I. Evil ones caused this planet to be destroyed by playing on the minds and the actions of its inhabitants, whose wavelength, like our own, had become slowed down so that they could not hear God. That terrible event took place long before our own planet was inhabited by man, but its repercussions were felt throughout our Solar System, the moon being the worst affected; this is now demonstrated by those vast 'craters', some of which are even visible to the human eye, which were caused by the bombardment of its surface by giant fragments of Uranus I. These were captured by Moon's gravitation, and as Moon, which itself had suffered at the instigation of the evil ones, had no atmosphere, these rocks did not burn up on entry into Moon's field of gravity. Mars too suffered in the same way, as did its moons, one of which is in fact nothing more than a great mass of rock flung from its unfortunate neighbouring planet at its final disintegration. The planet was blown asunder by forces only just coming to be understood on Earth, which forces, he said, man is no more capable of coping with now than he was on Uranus I.

I felt a shudder go through my whole being as I realised the full significance of his words.

He also mentioned that the planet Jupiter had acquired two more moons, following the explosion, as a result of its massive force of gravity. Earth itself, by then solid matter, had received a

portion of the ill–fated planet. This has since come to be
regarded as a meteor from outer space which buried itself deep
into the ground, causing a vast rift to be formed, the whole of
which has been regarded with awe ever since by the human
race, and given rise to much speculation and many erroneous
theories.

8

Child Refugees

On my next mission I found myself in a small room, sparsely furnished, and ill–lit by only one window. An open door, masked by a beaded curtain, led into what appeared to me to be a shop, for I could see goods neatly stacked and the end of a counter.

However, I had hardly taken stock of my surroundings before my Mentor spoke.

'This country is experiencing civil war with its attendant tragedies. Hiding under the table are two young children. Their mother's body lies behind the counter, although they do not know it. Insurgents tried to force her into disclosing the whereabouts of her husband. She refused, and was shot. The children terrified by the noise, took refuge and were not observed by the cursory glance given this inner room. You are to lead them out of the city and up a mountainside to where an old priest lives in seclusion. There they can take up temporary abode. The boy has been there before, when herding goats.'

I saw at once how it was that the children had been overlooked by their persecutors, for a long cloth hung over the table and almost down to the floor.

'Come!' I said, 'for those rough men have gone, but they may come back, so you must leave the house quickly by the back.' (I did not want them to find their dead mother.)

To my relief the boy emerged, telling his sister to follow. He did not see me but I believe he heard me.

'You must leave at once, before you are found. There is a good old priest who lives up the mountain path and he will help you.' Again I thought the boy had heard me. Taking his sister by the hand, he hurried out of the back entrance without going into the shop, to my intense relief.

'Tell them to keep to small side streets, or they may be recognised as the children of the wanted man.'

Again I passed this on to the boy. He looked about him fearfully, and clutching his sister's hand rushed the poor little thing down quiet alleys and side streets evidently well known to him. I judged him to be about twelve. Finally we reached the outskirts of the city, and he made his way purposefully up a well-worn path up a hillside.

The little girl was in tears by now, protesting that she wanted to go home.

'What, and have those men take you prisoner?' said her brother.

At this she quietened, and struggled on bravely. I lent her what strength I could, for the path was becoming increasingly stony and difficult.

At length we reached what might be termed a natural terrace on the mountainside, and here had been built a small stone chapel, with the priest's living quarters against it. Standing clear of both was a tall cross made of wood and quite rough in texture. It stood out boldly against the evening sky as the children paused close to it and looked down on to the city below, which now appeared to be on fire in certain areas. Almost at once the old priest emerged from the chapel, and after a few words of explanation from the boy, and tearful phrases from the little girl, he took them into his care.

'You may leave now,' said my Mentor. *'They will be safe with him until the situation below has stabilised and relatives claim them.'*

So I was withdrawn from the scene, taking a clear memory of these two waifs standing on the mountainside and being approached by the benign old priest in his long habit.

After I had been sent on several missions as an initiated knight I was summoned to attend my Master and beloved teacher, whose wisdom and kindly understanding ways I greatly revered, and once more I found myself sitting on the quaintly carved stool which he always set before him.

'My child,' he said in warmest tones, 'I have received high commendations with regard to your manner of handling the various complex situations to which you are sent on the material plane of existence where God the Great One's children are set at most risk. This is due to their vulnerability whilst forced to operate on a lower electrical speed than He had ever intended, as a result of the defection of His Archangel Satanaku, whose action He might not arrest owing to the law of freewill which operates throughout the Universe.'

I felt myself glowing with pleasure on hearing the approbation from my Master, who must in turn have received reports from my Mentors. However, this pleasurable sensation was not to last long, for my Master continued, 'At the same time, my child, I am informed that there is a certain element of impetuosity, sometimes amounting to impatience, to be discerned in your character. In order to increase your value as a member of The Company of White Knights, – your considerable value, I may say, my child,' (and here I felt he was encouraging me on account of my downcast looks, for I recognised the truth of his criticism, remembering at the same time how often from childhood onwards I had been chided for these same faults), 'you are to be sent on missions of a most demanding nature, where action of a less physical type is required. Instead, you will find yourself pitting your will against incarnate ones whose stubborn resistance to the ways of God has been implanted in their minds by the servants of the force of evil. These incarnate ones, be they men or women, have within them great potential in that they are generally highly evolved beings who have in past lives mastered many lessons and arts; it is for this very reason that they have become targets for the evil ones. Rather than see these talents and skills put to good use for the benefit of mankind and therefore to the delight of God the Great One, they were marked down from birth to be led astray and have implanted within their minds those lowered electrical beams, so that the evil entities assigned to this task might dictate their instructions and false precepts direct, from childhood onward. In this way it was ensured that these mortals might never use their potentially useful powers in the service of God the Great One. On the contrary they would be slowly but surely utilized to further the ends of their wicked masters. You, my son, will now be sent to certain of these unfortunate incarnate beings in order to counteract the powers of the evil ones and transplant into their minds the wishes and the precepts of the Great One Himself. This work, I must warn you, is of an extremely arduous character and few can sustain it for any length of time, so that they are withdrawn from the scene for a period of rest and, where necessary, a course of instruction from their tutors, such as I am giving you now, my son.' Here my Master paused, to smile benignly on me. 'But eventually you will be returned to the scene, or another of a similar nature, although the circumstances may be entirely different. Is there anything you wish to ask, my son?' he finished.

'Can you tell me, o, my Master, is there any way in which I can curb my impatient nature, which I recognise as having been inherent in my character ever since my childhood?'

Smiling indulgently, he replied, 'Only by the method of imposing on yourself a stern self-discipline will you find that ultimately you will have gained a complete mastery of your emotions.'

I thanked my dear Master for all he had told me and prepared to leave, for already I heard the voice of my Mentor telling me to report to the Great Hall, as I told my Master, although I believe he himself had received the same message. He rose, and embracing me warmly told me I might repair to him whenever I wanted advice.

9

The Attempt to Avoid War

Reaching the Great Hall I found I was instructed to join a small group of knights, of both sexes, who stood by themselves close to one of the tall windows from which could be seen the beautiful gardens laid outside. Smilingly they greeted me and I saw that I had worked with one or two of them already, on various missions.

Before I could make myself known, my Mentor spoke. *'You are to go on a most important mission, for the fate of a nation hangs on your success. The man whose mind you are to impress is debating within himself as to whether or not he will advocate war with a neighbouring state. He knows full well that his henchmen will follow him, for their very existence depends on him alone; but he is uncertain of the reaction of the populace, and fears revolt. His motives are purely selfish ones, for his mind is completely dominated by his evil masters. Upon arrival, (he will be in his own home,) you must station yourselves closely about, for his evil masters will not be visible, since they are relying entirely on the strong telepathic link which they have established with him from his earliest childhood days. You are to break this link by the force of prayer and a request to God that he may be purified of this unholy taint, so that his undoubted gifts of leadership be put to good use instead of bad. Nevertheless, you must be forever on your guard against the sudden attack of your opponents, who will inevitably strike back when they find they are being thwarted.'*

Having received these instructions, we found ourselves transported to a small but opulently furnished room, where sat a thickset middle-aged man who appeared to be deep in thought as he reviewed certain papers on a table before him. His hands were clenched as they lay on these papers, and his whole attitude denoted a repressed dynamism, as though he longed to spring into action but a certain inherent streak of caution held him back.

'Surround him as you were directed, and pray to God that he may be insulated from the telepathic links formed by his unholy masters,' instructed my Mentor, and I could tell that my colleagues had received the same message, for we immediately formed a tight circle about this unfortunate man; furniture and suchlike objects proving to be of no obstacle to us, who were operating in a different dimension and on a different 'wavelength'.

At the same time I prayed to God that this man's mind might be freed from the shackles laid on him by our opponents, and speaking to him from our dimension I said, *'Think well before you act, my friend, for the fate of thousands of your fellow countrymen depends on your decision. Do you wish to bring destruction and misery to the land of your birth? And to what end? Self-aggrandisement is no valid reason for such action as you are debating within yourself.'*

All at once the man sprang up from his chair, exclaiming as he did so, *'A-ah!'* in tones of great perturbation.

'You have touched his better self,' said my Mentor. *'Continue along those same lines, but beware of your opponents' reaction.'*

As he paced about we kept in close contact with him, taking it in turns to speak to his better self. This we did by means of our own telepathic communication. Finally it appeared that he had reached some decision, for he strode back to his chair and reached for that instrument that I now know to be named a telephone; but before he could speak into it I became increasingly aware of a sense of drowsiness and unreality, so that my surroundings and even my dear colleagues' faces seemed to be melting away.

'Cry to God for help!' came my Mentor's voice in most peremptory tones. *'You are being attacked by extremely powerful forces.'*

Summoning my will power with utmost difficulty I said, mentally of course, 'Please help us God,' and upon the instant a shaft of light shone down into the room, imbuing us with a sense of love and reassurance. At once our surroundings appeared to me exactly as they had before, and my colleagues once more came into focus. I could tell by their expressions that they too had undergone this same horrific experience.

'Follow up your momentary respite,' my Mentor told me. *'Advise this man to improve the wretched lifestyle of the majority of his people, rather than seek to lead them to destruction at the hands of their neighbours.'*

At this, I renewed my attempts to influence this man who held the lives of so many thousands in his hands, whilst my colleagues bent their wills to hold back the messages which were undoubtedly being relayed into his mind by the forces of evil.

I spoke to him. 'You have the capabilities to lead your fellowmen. Use this gift to their advantage, and not to your own selfish interest. If you do not, you will have a stain of guilt upon your soul which will require several lives on Earth to expunge. Think hard, my friend, before you load yourself with this appalling debt to humanity.' Once again he sat before his desk and reached out for his telephone, which before he had refrained from using.

'Do not relax your concentration for one instant,' said the voice of my Mentor, *'for you have gained ground, and his next action will be crucial to your success.'*

'Cancel your warlike manoeuvres,' I said, speaking as urgently as I was able under the circumstances. 'Do not stop for second thoughts, or it may be too late. Already the neighbouring state is aware of your intentions and is mustering its forces to repel you.'

A moment later I recognised my blunder, for he withdrew his hand from the telephone, and my Mentor said,

'You have but stiffened his resolve to teach them a lesson as he would put it. Try another approach at once.'

Much disheartened, I said, 'They are well aware too that their forces are inferior to yours, and are merely making a show of arms to hearten their people. If you refrain from attacking they will merely be making themselves a laughing-stock in the eyes of the world, and you will gain all the more approbation for your forbearance.'

This time I felt myself to be on safer ground, and, moreover, I gained the impression that he was indeed receiving my messages. He leapt to his feet and, opening a door to an inner office, revealed to us the startled faces of some men who sat there before massive machines which I knew to be radio receivers of some sort. These men wore headphones attached to the machines, and one man, removing his, stood to attention.

'Sir,' he said, 'we are receiving reports that there are troops massing troops beyond our frontier. The inhabitants living in that area are becoming alarmed and seek assurance that they are to be protected.'

Quickly I intervened, 'Tell them, there is no need to fear, for their neighbours are well aware that they are the weaker nation, and therefore will not be the first to make a provocative move.' I spoke with great firmness and severity.

There was no doubt this time that he had heard me, for he uttered a loud sardonic laugh and said, 'What, do they fear our neighbour's little pipsqueac army? Tell them I could wipe it out within a day. And', he added, 'they deceive themselves if they imagine I would waste time and money in overpowering such a petty little country. Rather I would set to work improving the lot of our own people.'

'Well done!' I cried, enthusiastically, 'bravo, my friend, you have taken the right line. Now enumerate some of the ways in which you will help your people.'

'Those roads you keep on asking for shall be built, and, where necessary, houses— — —'

Here he broke off, for there was a loud knock on the door of his own office, and when he called out in answer a man in military uniform came hurrying in, carrying a sheaf of maps and written orders, as I recognised from my own military days, even though their appearance was of a different nature in some respects. Saluting smartly he spoke to our charge in brisk phrases, saying that all was in readiness for the campaign to begin, and that he only required the final command to set it in motion. My heart sank, for I feared that this would be the most formidable challenge of all.

'Speak to him sternly,' said my Mentor. *'Tell him he was not summoned to his superior and had no business to break in on his deliberations, which moreover had reached a climax, for he was not prepared to embark on this bloodthirsty campaign.'*

I did as I was told immediately, using all the vigour I could command in my delivery.

My words appeared to have some effect, for the general, as I assume he was, fell back a pace or two saying, 'But I am interrupting your work of sustaining the nation with— — — '

Here our statesman spoke firmly and with assurance, breaking in on his minion's words. 'You are indeed interrupting my work. But you may hear my latest decision. I do *not* intend incurring the loss of life such a campaign would undoubtedly bring about for the end merely of subjugating so petty a nation. You may turn the campaign into a large-scale manoeuvre, along the lines of our annual exercises. I shall supervise it myself.'

Upon this unexpected announcement the general looked aghast, and stepping impetuously forward he exclaimed, 'Your Excellency, all is prepared. Your men are straining at the leash! How can I tell them all these preparations are for nothing? They will not believe me!'

'Reprimand him for insubordination,' I instructed our statesman, as quickly and as firmly as I could.

'Then if you will not obey my orders, General, I shall tell them myself,' he said, turning towards the door.

'Act upon your words,' I commanded him sternly.

'Excellency, I must ask you to reconsider your decision. The eyes of the world are upon us. We shall be branded as cowards. Already we have been termed your "toy soldiers" by foreigners who relay news to their countries.' The General looked quite apoplectic with indignation as he announced this, whilst the effect it had on our charge was immediate. He halted by the door, his eyes blazed with fury, and I felt all was lost.

'Are you going to listen to such nonsense?' I cried hotly, 'and coming from one who should be subordinate to you?'

The cool voice of my Mentor spoke in my ear: *'We are removing you from this mission, and replacing you with another. You have done well so far but your patience has been tried to its limits.'*

On this I found myself instantly transported to the cloister, wherein I knew I should find the door of my dear Master. Knocking on it I was immediately told to enter. Crestfallen and ashamed I hurried to my stool, and wordlessly sat before him, my head between my hands. Soon I felt a kind hand rest on my shoulder as though to reassure me.

'My child,' said my Master, 'do not be so downcast. Your Mentor reports to me that you led your party and handled the situation in a most exemplary manner, so that it was only when the forces of evil manipulated to your extreme disadvantage, just as you were on the verge of success, that your emotions overcame you, and it was deemed wisest to replace you by one who is more experienced in opposing the enemy. Do not distress yourself, for you have done well, and have prepared the ground for the one who succeeded you.'

With this he returned to his elaborately carved chair, and I sprang to my feet, exclaiming apologies for my lack of decorum when entering his room. Belatedly I bowed, and he, acknowledging my apology, indicated that I should once more sit, although I must first immerse myself in his pool. This I did, thanking him for his words of encouragement.

He then outlined to me certain methods of handling such situations as I have described, enjoining me not to become too closely implicated in the project on hand, but rather to view it objectively and not as though I were a participant. Furthermore, he said that I should continually bear in mind that the enemy, the force of evil, will inevitably strike back with counter-measures when some ground has been gained by God's servants; it should come as no surprise when this takes place, which may possibly be just when you are anticipating victory.' He added that I should always remember that I could summon help where I considered it necessary by requesting it of my Mentor, or in fact from God Himself.

Following on this discourse, my Master rose and led me kindly into his garden where, he said, the beauty of its many features would help me to compose myself after the stress of contending with so powerful a foe. Having walked in its shady avenues and admired its many vistas we sat for a while on our customary seat, whilst he instructed me as to the names of the various trees and plants around us, which were for the most part unfamiliar to me since thet were of a tropical nature.

As we sat in harmony with one another and with our surroundings, I received a message from my Mentor, telling me to report once more for duty. I stood, and thanked my Master for his reassurance and help, and I could tell that he too had received this message. Bowing, I left him and hurried to the Great Assembly Hall where I found several of my colleagues grouped together, although my uncle was not there. We stood in a circle, each listening to our own Mentor.

10

Foiling Mercenary Exploiters

I heard my Mentor say, *'You will be sent to people of a simple, unevolved culture, who are in danger of being exploited by a ruthless consortium whose sole objective is to make money with no regard as to the welfare of the indigenous population. It is our wish that you influence the mind of the Headman, or Chieftain, to refuse to accept the blandishments of these mercenary men, who are undoubtedly being used by the evil ones. Tell him that the gifts they offer are of little use to his people, magical though they may seem to be; that they will not last, nor will his people know how to repair them, and that his people will prosper far better without the intrusion of these strangers, who will despoil the land in the search for the commodity they desire. Besides which, they will disrupt the harmony of his society and even bring disease with them, if he consents to let them come. You will find these people more receptive to your words than are those of most other societies, for they have remained close to the natural order of God's ways.'*

After hearing our instructions we found ourselves transported to a scene which at first seemed in every way idyllic, for a calm blue sea lapped peacefully on to smooth sandy beaches, whilst over our heads waved feathery leaves on tall, slender trunks shading the people below from a brightly shining sun. We soon saw, however, that the servants of the enemy of man were there before us; dark shapes, now familiar to us all, stood behind those who were evidently strangers to the land; they were dressed in conventional western clothing compared to the natives, who wore very little and who were dark-skinned.

'Stand behind the Headman or Chief,' my Mentor told me, *'and impress him with the thought that these strangers, for all their fair words, are not to be trusted.'*

Immediately I went to him who was obviously the chief, for he sat on a rudely, constructed seat flanked by stalwart warriors, holding strong cudgels or spears, whose looks showed that they were not to be taken lightly.

'Send these strangers away from your land,' I said as decisively as I was able. 'They will only do harm to your people. No good will come from any dealings with them.'

I felt sure that my man heard me, for he turned his head momentarily in my direction, and then spoke to the one who was evidently acting as interpreter and who sat cross-legged between the two groups.

'We do not need your goods, and we do not wish to trade with you. Go now in peace, for I have nothing more to say to you.'

At this the leader of the strangers' party became very irate and, raising his voice, he spoke angrily, saying that he could not go away empty-handed, for his own 'chief' had sent him on this mission; there were certain products on this island that he badly needed and he had no intention of going without them even if he had to take them by force! At this, he waved a weapon in his hand.

When the interpreter had finished I quickly interposed before this ugly situation deteriorated. 'Pay no attention to his threats, for he is merely trying to frighten you. Tell him to seek this product on another island where no one lives, and that what is to be found on this island belongs by right to you and to your people.'

To my intense gratification my friend the Chieftain repeated what I had said to him (in my own language) in his own language, and with tones of great authority in his voice.

This means of telepathic communication still had powers to surprise me, but my Mentor urged me to press home my point.

'Tell him to leave, or you will sink his boat.'

Immediately he repeated my instructions, at which, as I had feared, the foreigner showed his intentions of becoming dangerous; signalling to one of his men, who at once stepped forward he pointed to a brightly coloured bird which had perched in a tree above us, and the interpreter in rising tones of fear said,

'He says that what is done to that bird will be done to all of you if you do not fall in with his wishes!' whereupon the marksman took aim, a shot rang out, and the poor bird fell dead at our feet.

I seized the opportunity to speak, in the shocked silence

which followed this act of violence. 'Order your men to take charge of the boat which brought them to shore, saying that it will be sunk if they do not consent to leave, and then they will have no means of regaining their ship; remind them that these are shark, infested waters.'

The chief immediately issued commands to his men, and a dozen or so emerged from the shadows of the trees and in no time had taken possession of the strangers' craft which lay, gently rocking, just offshore made fast to a convenient outcrop onshore.

'Speak to the leader of the intruders,' my Mentor told me, 'telling him they can hole his boat, leaving him and his companions stranded amidst a hostile people. Your colleagues will accompany you, for you must first banish the forces of darkness who are overshadowing him.'

So intent had been my concentration on the Chief, behind whom I had found myself standing on arrival, that I must confess I had forgotten the dark figures who stood close beside the party of visitors., My colleagues had received the same instructions, I could tell, for they moved forward with me and approaching these sinister presences we bent our will against theirs. I know that I myself issued a heartfelt prayer to God for help. On the instant a beam of light, unseen by the human beings present, shone down on to our opponents, who instantly fell back with unearthly cries of pain. They seemed to melt away before our eyes, translated I imagine by their evil masters to some other sphere, or perhaps sent to torment some other poor mortals elsewhere.

The morale of the invading party melted too, and their leader, sensing that his authority was undermined and that there was a growing apprehension amongst his men, who muttered uneasily together, made a conciliatory speech to the Chief, saying that there was no need to sink his boat, for if he would order his men to relinquish it, they would embark and, taking his advice, seek another island, where no one lived. This was interpreted rapidly by the poor man who was in their pay, and who had sprung to his feet in alarm at the earlier exchanges, feeling his own life to be in danger.

We were not recalled immediately, for our Mentors told us that we were to remain where we were until the area had been cleansed of the baleful influence of the evil ones. This operation is performed by a number of God's Angel Host who are directed to the area which we mortal souls are guarding, and who are especially trained in this work. As we stood on guard, concentrating our minds on repelling the force of evil who would instantly have taken advantage of the situation had we relaxed, for the heavenly beam of light covered only a small area, we became aware of the strangers embarking in their craft and retreating to the ship, which lay at anchor in the bay.

However, almost at once the Angel Band appeared before us and we watched these dedicated beings at their work. They crossed and recrossed the whole area in question, holding their hands out before them, palms downward, and we knew that God's invisible rays were being directed through them and deep into the heart of the world. When they had finished we were withdrawn from the scene, and we found ourselves back in the Great Hall, our mission accomplished.

11

The Peace Conference

The next mission I propose to relate was of an altogether different nature, for we were sent to a Concourse of Nations who were supposedly discussing peace plans aimed at removing all threats of warfare from the world. Our Mentors stationed us behind the chief protagonists in this battle of wills, and at the same time warned us of the close proximity of the servants of the force, of evil, who would oppose all attempts to bring about a successful conclusion to this conference.

'*Be forever on your guard against the powerful electric forces at the disposal of your opponents, and at the very first symptom of a certain numbing of your senses you must immediately request help from God, who will then succour you with His counteracting forces. The object of this conference is ostensibly to reassure the majority of the world's nations that their elected leaders are indeed seeking to maintain peace, and to curtail the manufacture of deadly weapons and other means of destroying their fellow humankind; but in point of fact they have no intention whatsoever of limiting their supply of armaments within their own countries; where possible they also wish to purvey these armaments to other countries; with the object of obtaining credit and power over unfortunate smaller countries.*

'*The minds of those present are for the most part already attuned to the force, of evil, who are thus enabled to transmit their wicked plans direct to them; the part you have to play is to concentrate your mind on the mortals to whom you have been assigned that, by so doing, you break the link already established with the evil force, and when this has been achieved you can then direct God's wishes to them instead. This will not be easy, for they have long been indoctrinated by this same force, as have their predecessors, so that their long established mode of conducting international affairs and, above all, international finance appears to them to be immutable. You must recognise this, for it will prove to be*

*your greatest stumbling block, and until you are able to introduce into
their minds the idea that the old methods are outdated and are therefore
no longer viable in the world as it is at present, you will make no
progress. When there is a glimmering of doubt within the mind of him
who sits before you, I will tell you; then you must redouble your
concentration, at the same time instilling a new train of thought into
him; suggest that other theories should be explored before plunging the
world even deeper into the morass of greed and of suspicion of other
nations' motives, and the ever, present pressure to manufacture more
armaments as a means of providing work for the masses.'*

At this, I concentrated my attention on this man before me
who was, I soon discovered, a native of France, so that I realised
why I had been assigned to him, since I have chosen to manifest
in my incarnation as Jacques de la Court in that country, albeit
under very different circumstances from those of the twentieth
century. Nevertheless, there would be sure to be a certain
affinity between us. He was, I soon made out, an extremely
stubborn man and, at any slight suggestion of what he and I
should term a 'rapprochement' between the different representatives; he instinctively opposed it, scarcely waiting to hear the
other participants' views. I observed that his translators tactfully
toned down his somewhat vehement expressions, so that only
those who understood French knew exactly what he was saying;
but his tone of voice left the others in no doubt.

I tried speaking to him, telepathically of course. 'My friend,' I
said, 'you are here to promote peace, not disharmony. At least
you should listen to those suggestions your fellowmen are
putting forward.'

For the moment I had the idea he had heard me, for he turned
at once to look over his shoulder, and moved uncomfortably in
his chair.

'Well done,' spoke the voice of my Mentor, *'you have made some
impact. Continue along those lines. He is a lawyer, and trained to listen
to the other's point of view.'*

I repeated my words, more emphatically this time, but there
was no visible reaction. However, I decided to press home my
point, and I reminded him that he was trained to give a fair
hearing to all parties concerned.

The result was quite startling, for this man, this delegate so
obdurate at first, suddenly underwent a complete change of
attitude, and to the surprise of all he made an open apology for

his last comments, further announcing that it was only fair that all the delegates should be given a hearing. You cannot imagine my sense of elation, for not only had he taken my advice but he had used almost the selfsame words that I had spoken into his mind, so that I felt I had forged a strong link with him.

But my Mentor's voice spoke quite sharply in my ears: *'Do not relax your concentration. You have done well so far, but nevertheless his mind is still attuned to the force of evil, whose servants will undoubtedly try to cancel out the advantage you have gained.'*

With this warning in my ears I renewed my concentration, at the same time evolving in my mind a new line of approach. This man, M. Bertrand, although in fact I did not know his name, would almost certainly have been brought up in the Roman Catholic religion, and I intended to remind him of his early teaching.

'You are a Christian,' I said in firm tones. 'You should love your neighbour, whatever his race or nationality. It is not right that you connive in, or even countenance, the manufacture and purveyance of the means of slaughtering fellow human beings. Is this the love that our Saviour brought into the world?'

I had no means of telling whether my words were registering within his conscience, since he remained quiescent. At the same time I became aware within myself of a certain sense of lethargy, and knew that my concentration was slipping. I redoubled my efforts to regain it, but felt it was to no avail.

All at once my Mentor spoke. *'Pray to God instantly, for you are in danger of being overcome by the force of the enemy.'*

At once I sent up a prayer to God, asking that I be protected from the powers of evil. Immediately I felt a release from the sluggishness which had been creeping over me in an insidious manner, and that I was once more quite alert and in full command of my senses.

Having had this alarming experience, I resolved to be even more on my guard against the very first symptoms of an attack, and once again I set to work on my appointed task.

'Remember,' I said to M. Bertrand, 'it is not merely the future of your fellow countrymen but the future of the peoples of the whole world which is at stake. Our Lord Jesus brought love into the world, not mistrust or hostility towards other nations. You were taught this in the days of your youth. Do not forget these God–given precepts, now that you are in a position of great responsibility; on account of your sound judgement and many other talents as a lawyer your people have elected you to represent them, and they trust you to protect their interests.'

My charge became very thoughtful, almost to the point of seeming abstracted; I sensed an inner turmoil taking place within his mind, so I took the opportunity of sending a prayer to God that He might change the heart of His child who had obviously been receiving instructions from the servants of the force of evil, since they had retaliated so promptly when he showed signs of responding to my directions and my words of advice.

The result of my appeal to God was apparent to all, for my charge gave a great sigh, and leaning forward he held his head in his hands, his elbows on the table before him.

'M. Bertrand is unwell,' murmured those about him, whilst some offered him aid.

'No, no!' he exclaimed, 'I thank you, but I am perfectly well. It is the complexities of the problems before us which overwhelm me from time to time. Please continue with the debate.'

My Mentor congratulated me on my handling of the situation, and told me to continue along the same lines.

I spoke again into my charge's inner mind: 'Announce your views to the other participants of this conference, for upon the outcome will depend the welfare and indeed the lives of many thousands of your fellow men.'

No sooner had I given him this telepathic message than he rose to his feet and proceeded to make a most telling speech, invoking the sympathy of those present for the great masses of world population who were attempting to exist in dire poverty and under utterly degrading conditions. I sensed an astonished reaction within the conference hall to this so unexpected plea from one whom they had considered to be a trustworthy supporter of the present regime and mode of transacting commerce in the twentieth century.

'You must give him all the support you can,' my Mentor told me, *for he is confronted by the most powerful cartel known to exist on Earth, and they will not allow any interference with their age-old methods of conducting commerce. Nor do they feel the slightest pity for the unfortunate masses. He will stand alone against these all powerful ones, and will undoubtedly be brought down at their instigation, both in his*

*private and in his public life, unless we are able to rouse some support
from other members of this conference. We are going to place one of your
colleagues behind this man to maintain the progress you have made,
whilst you endeavour to enlist the support of those who already find
themselves in sympathy with him.'*

At this I found myself transported to another part of the
Council Chamber, some distance away, where I stood behind
the chair of a man whose origin seemed to me to be Asiatic, and
in fact my Mentor told me that he came from Burma and that he
was a deeply religious man of the Buddhist faith.

'Speak up, my friend,' I said to him telepathically. 'Pronounce
your views in support of him who has made so humane a plea
for your fellow men, just as the great Lord Buddha did some
thousands of years ago.'

I watched my new charge intently and saw him give a visible
start, even turning to look behind him as though expecting to
see someone standing there. But his eyes looked straight through
me as I stood, living on another dimension as I was. Nevertheless, I felt that he must have gathered the gist of my message,
and I was encouraged.

'This man is psychic,' said my Mentor; *'press home your point.'*

'Speak up before it is too late,' I told him, 'and the enemies of
God talk him down.'

Immediately this man stood up and spoke in his own
language which I could tell was being translated on the spot by
some mechanical device with which I am unfamiliar, but which
was understood by all, as I could see by their faces. He gave a
most graphic and telling description of some of the needs in
certain areas of his own society.

'Well done!' said my Mentor, and I found myself behind yet
another delegate to the conference.

'Here,' I was told, *'is a die-hard of the old order. Speak to him
firmly, and if necessary repeat your words with utmost regularity, until
you see signs that he is hearing you. Remind him that he was always
taught to love his neighbour as himself.'*

At once I concentrated my attention on the man before me,
and taking my Mentor's advice I reminded him of the law,
'Love thy neighbour as thyself'. To begin with I sensed an air of
anger and resentment, added to which was a certain feeling of
fear and apprehension, as he listened to the outspoken
sentiments being voiced by other delegates. Several times he

ejaculated phrases of strong disapproval as the general tenor of opinion followed the more humanitarian lines engendered by my first two charges. However, as I continued to repeat that great commandment 'Love thy neighbour', as recommended to me by my Mentor, a visible change came over this man before me. He showed signs of great agitation, running his finger round his collar as though it had become too tight, pressing his hand to his forehead, and moving restlessly in his seat. Finally he took up a pen and scribbled hurriedly on the paper before him. This he passed to his immediate neighbour, who read it with expression of astonishment amounting to disbelief on his face.

'He has made the suggestion that certain large sums of money be released for the purpose of helping those countries under discussion. You have done well. Now repeat your method with the men sitting on either side of him.'

At once I moved behind the man to whom my charge had passed the paper, and began to repeat the same commandment telepathically and with utmost monotony. It seemed to me that I was making no impression whatsoever on this man, until I interpolated, 'This is the law of God', before continuing with my repetition.

The scowl left his face and in its place there came an air of cool calculation, as of someone working out a problem within his mind.

It was at this point that events took a dramatic turn, for he who had first written down his suggestions, and passed them to his neighbour, gave a sudden gasp, then clutching his chest with his right hand he attempted to rise, but fell forward on to the table in front of him in a state of collapse.

At once a doctor was called for; the delegates nearest to him hastened to his side, and the meeting was in total disarray.

'He is dead,' my Mentor told me. *'The servants of the evil ones have no mercy; they saw in him a weak link in the chain that binds mankind, and by manipulating the electric forces at their command they worked upon his weak heart, for which he was already undergoing treatment.'*

A feeling of intense dismay overcame me. 'Then,' I cried, 'by my action I brought about this man's death! Are the forces of God not stronger than the forces of evil, that they can take the life of His child?'

'Not on a planet so severely infiltrated by their power as is planet

Earth. It is better for this man's soul that he should die with his last action being one of compassion to make some small reparation for all the strictures he has inflicted on society during the rest of his life. We are withdrawing you now from this scene, for the conference will now be adjourned. Rest assured you have done well.'

12

Helping those who Maintain Law

On my next mission I was again sent to help the forces of law and order, in a situation of extreme violence in that country of my origin as Jacques de la Court.

'Here we have men of low calibre,' said my Mentor, *'who have spent few mortal lives on Earth, and who are therefore all the more easily influenced by the forces of evil, whom you will see all about you as dark forms, so that you must be forever on your guard. In fact, you will do well to remain in a close formation so that not one of you can be singled out as their prey.'*

At this, I noticed that my colleagues must be receiving the same message as myself, since they all drew together in a compact group, I joining them.

'We have placed you behind those men whose duty it is to protect the citizens of this town from the dangers inherent in anarchy. These men are of an altogether higher evolutionary status but nevertheless they are being attacked by larger numbers, and may easily resort to violence themselves out of the need for self-defence. This is exactly what the force of evil desires in order to donigrate the law, whilst at the same time inflaming those who are rebelling against it still further. Your role is to strengthen the resolve and courage of the men of law by mental encouragement, whilst at the same time others of your friends will engage themselves in the attempt to deflect the missiles, by means of certain electrical forces we are supplying for that purpose.' At once I could grasp the gravity of the situation, for the dark forces had so lowered the wavelength in that area that it gave me such a sense of acute discomfort that I found it extremely difficult to formulate any plan whatsoever.

However, I concentrated on the men directly before me, saying, 'Courage, mes braves, for the force of God is behind you, and He will not permit His children to suffer at the hands of these ruffians.'

I believe one man heard me as though I were a mortal, for he turned for a brief moment to look over his shoulder, and I was able to glimpse the fear in his eyes. At that moment a stone struck him on the helmet, but it fell harmlessly to the ground.

'The angels of God are here to help you,' I said. (I referred to "angels" rather than to the "White Knights", about whom he would know nothing.) 'You yourself must send up a prayer to God for protection, for our powers on Earth are limited by the Devil.' (I spoke in the terminology of his religion.) I had directed my thoughts specifically at that man who had turned, but I was gratified to see that not only he but his comrade to the right of him had heard, and sent out a prayer to the Almighty. Upon the instant two bright beams of light were directed on to them from above, unseen by them but clearly visible to us. Moreover, the enemy themselves not only saw them but felt the instantaneous effect of the higher rate of the electrical forces operating there, and with weird howls of rage and pain they reacted immediately, and I saw some fall back from their posts behind the insurrectionists.

'Well done,' said my Mentor; 'the heat has gone from the situation. Nevertheless, the battle is not won. Continue along those lines.'

In order to do so I moved to another position, where I could see that those who attempted to maintain order were being hard-pressed by the unseen forces of the enemy, and I signalled to some of my comrades to accompany me, since it is never safe to isolate oneself, for fear of being captured. Here we found ourselves in the thick of an affray between our charges and those rough men who were allowing themselves to be manipulated by the forces of evil, whose dark presences were to be seen on every hand. Keeping close to one another, we advanced into the centre of the turmoil and there we formed a tight group, backs together and facing outwards so that we might not be taken unawares. Shrieks of fury raged about us from the dark entities, unheard of course by man; and the numbing sensation, with which I had now become familiar, began to creep over us, as the enemy directed their full hatred on us.

'Pray to God for help,' said the voice of my Mentor in my inner ear, 'or you will be overpowered.'

This I did at once, and immediately a brilliant beam of light was directed between us and the dark forces. The unbearable tension was relaxed and we felt normal, whilst at the same time our enemy fell back uttering now not shrieks of anger, but of pain and dismay. We advanced on them, telling them to go back whence they came and admonishing them nevermore to torment or lead astray God's children. As we did this we saw that the human insurrectionists were also falling back, as though they had lost all heart in their enterprise and were wondering how they might emerge from it without being taken into custody, since those who upheld the law were pressing home their advantage and seeking out likely ring-leaders. Nevertheless, we remained where we were, all the members of our group gathered close together and protected by the steady beam of light directed on to us from above; for we feared that the opposition might return, in an attempt to muster its forces once again; besides which, our Mentors had not recalled us.

As we stood there I prayed that this place might be protected from the forces of darkness, nevermore to be used by them.

A wonderfully loving voice answered me, and I knew it to be the voice of God Himself. 'You have done well, my dearest child, to make this intercession, for by doing so you have enabled me to render this place safe for my children for evermore. Remember to do this whenever the occasion arises. Blessings on you, my dearest child.'

I stood quite spellbound for the moment, until a colleague said, 'Come, Jacques, we are bidden to return. Our task here is over. Did you not hear your Mentor?'

Turning to my friend I must have looked somewhat bewildered, for she took my hand and led me closer still to the others, and upon the instant we were transported back to our Citadel.

13

The Lessons to be Learned on the Battlefront

On my next mission I and my colleagues found ourselves to be in a scene of such horror that I find it difficult to describe. On every hand there appeared to be thunderous explosions, the effects of which disturbed even our equilibrium; to the poor incarnate combatants it must have seemed quite intolerable. I found myself admiring their strength of will as I saw them carry out their orders under conditions which must have numbed their very senses, added to which they would have been well aware that every second might be their last, or that their physical self might be injured for life.

However, my Mentor did not allow me to dwell on the appalling scenes before me, beside which the battlefront in my own life in seventeenth century France seemed mere childsplay; he said, *'You are to go to him who is in command of the invading force and impress on his mind that the battle is lost for his compatriots, and that he must steel himself to surrender and thus end the unnecessary carnage and suffering on both sides. He stands with his subordinate officers behind a rocky outcrop to your right. Go to him at once for his resolve is being stiffened by an enemy of God.'*

Immediately I turned, to find this group of incarnate ones who spoke not only with one another, but also through some apparatus, such as I have seen used before in modern times, issuing instructions to their men. My colleagues had received the same message as myself, I could tell, for we all converged onto this group of officers and surrounded them. I could see at once who was in command, for standing close behind him was the dark figure who was the servant of the force of evil.

Confronting this loathsome entity I said, 'In the name of God I command you to go.'

It turned on me with a sneer on its grotesque features, and I could feel the full force of the power at its command being directed at me. At once I sent a prayer to God for help and on the instant a beam of light shone down, encircling the entire group. The effect on my protagonist was immediate, for it let out an unearthly shriek and disappeared before my eyes.

'Now speak to your man,' said my Mentor.

I stood before him, knowing nevertheless that he was unable to see me.

'You must surrender. The day is lost. By prolonging the battle you are only inflicting untold misery on God's children.'

'He wears a cross around his neck,' my Mentor said; *'remind him of his beliefs.'*

'Remember the word of God, "Thou shalt do no murder". Swallow your pride, my friend, and give in to your opponents. They will treat you with mercy.'

I saw doubt come into his eyes, and felt that he had heard at least some part of my message. Furthermore, at that point those who were stationed at the speaking apparatus turned and announced that things were going badly for his men; in fact, communications were failing. Reluctantly he told his subordinates that the time had come to surrender, and that this message must be sent to the opposing army leaders.

'Well done,' said my Mentor. *'You have achieved your end. We will withdraw you.'*

'But,' I cried, 'may we not go to the assistance of those who are dying, and sustain those who are wounded?' (for on all sides I was aware of mortal injury, fear and terrible suffering on the part of the fallen).

'No, that is not for you,' my Mentor said; and a great pity filled my heart. *'Their own Guides are helping them. Your work here is done.'*

And so I turned from the scene of carnage to regroup with my colleagues.

14

Quelling a Mob

On our next assignment we were sent to an angry situation where the workers in a certain industry had banded together in order to flout the authorities in their area. They considered that they had been very badly treated by those in charge of the concern and that their very livelihoods were at risk, and that both they and those dependent on them would be left without means. We were told that, although they had indeed cause for complaint and that little attention had been accorded their more peaceful attempt to find a solution to the problems, they were now acting under the influence of the evil ones who would ever set man against man, using the basest methods at their command. In this case we could see the dark figures over-shadowing those who were the ringleaders; we could tell that they were inciting them, and those who were their followers, to further and further acts of violence against those unfortunates who were there to maintain law and order, and who had no personal interest on either side.

It seemed to us that there was one particular man who was most successful in rousing the ire of the crowd and urging them to excesses, with his loud-mouthed almost hysterical way of addressing the men involved. He himself was clearly being influenced by one of the dark figures, which was plainly to be seen overshadowing him, to the extent that it must have been almost taking him over; by which I mean that it had banished the poor wretch's soul from his body so that it could make these foul utterances and blasphemies through his mouth.

By silent commune, I and my colleagues agreed to encircle this ringleader in order to banish the intruder. This we did immediately, whilst at the same time I said imperatively, 'Go! Go to your own place in the scheme of things, and leave this child of God to lead his own life peacefully.' I then prayed to God that His child might be freed of this unwelcome tyrant.

The result was instantaneous. We heard a most unearthly shriek and saw the dark one disengage itself from the man and rush from the scene, breaking through our rank between myself and my neighbouring comrade, whereupon we felt a most dreadful shiver go through us and sensed that something loathsome bordering on putrefaction had been near. Meanwhile, its luckless host, held in the ray of light from God, gave a few choking sounds and then sank to the ground, where he lay twitching and moaning lightly.

The effect on the crowd was electrifying, for they quietened at once and those who had been standing close to him now looked down at him as he lay helpless and emitting low groans.

'He's had a fit,' one said. 'Or a stroke,' said another; whilst a more compassionate one threw his coat over the still prostrate man.

'Tell them to keep back whilst he comes to his sense,' said my Mentor; and I tried to impress this message into thir minds.

Before long, those who had been sent to contain the riot and who had been sent word of this man's collapse, brought along a stretcher, to which he was transferred and removed from the scene, already showing signs of returning to his normal self.

'He's all right,' said one. 'I've seen this happen before. He gets properly worked up, and then all of a sudden he'll go out like a light, just as he did today. It's like two people in one.'

'He will be all right,' my Mentor told me; 'he merely requires a time of quiet in which to return to his own self. We want you to stay where you are, guarding this territory until the Angel Host come to cleans, this area, so that it may nevermore be visited by the destructive force.'

So we stood together in a group, concentrating our wills on the area in question, so that none of the enemy dare return; once again we watched those dedicated ones of the order of Angels as they went about their task of directing God's higher electrical forces into the very ground, in order to counteract the heavy electrical forces implanted there by the evil ones since time immemorial. Once again I watched these true servants of God as they worked, almost entranced, as it seemed to me, by their intense concentration on the matter in hand; wherever they went, a wonderful beam of light followed them. When they had finished their work they grouped together, and we sensed a great harmony between them. They appeared to be drawn up then into a beam of light and vanished from our sight.

Shortly afterwards we too were withdrawn from the scene, to find ourselves once more in the Great Hall of the Citadel of the White Knights.

15

Industrial Greed

On our next mission we found ourselves in what I knew to be called 'a factory', although of course there were no such places in my life as Jacques, nor indeed in my subsequent life. We saw on all sides giant pieces of machinery in motion, although none of them appeared to be similar, nor were they performing the same function so far as I could see; nevertheless there was a certain harmony about these machines, marred only by the perpetual noise they made. I noticed that the human beings who attended them were obliged to shout to one another if they wished to say anything.

'You will see a man standing on your right, whose work it is to sort the items as they reach him, discarding any faulty pieces he may see. It has been reported to us that he is in grave danger, owing to insufficient supervision of the machine he is operating. This we can tell you briefly is in turn due to the industrialist, who is in charge of the concern, having reduced his engineering staff in order that he may pay fewer wages and thereby gain more profit. Stand close beside this man and warn him to be on his guard, for there is danger.'

I went at once to the man on my right and said into his mind, 'Be on your guard, my friend, for your machine is dangerous.'

To my surprise he reacted immediately, for not only did he touch a switch which appeared to slow down the machinery, but he called out to another man, some way off, 'Here, have a look at this. I think there's a fault somewhere here.'

The other man, whom I assumed to be the foreman, hurried to the spot, took a quick look and ordered my friend to stop working on it, before going across to telephone a report.

Almost at once, all the machinery came to a halt.

Some men in overalls of a darker colour appeared, carrying tool boxes and examined the machine under suspicion. Very soon they seemed to find what they were looking for, and one turned to my friend saying, 'It's a good job you stopped when you did, mate, or you might have been electrocuted.'

'Well, that would have stopped me all right, wouldn't it!' My friend spoke jokingly, but he was visibly shaken. 'Funny thing,' he went on, 'I thought I heard Joe here warning me, and yet when I looked up, there he was, standing right over there.'

'It's all on account of the cut-down. These machines ought to be serviced more regularly same as they used to be,' answered the engineer, as he and the other worked at it.

'Tell the foreman to report this incident to his superiors making it clear that great danger is involved,' my Mentor instructed me.

I and my colleagues gathered round the man, unseen by him of course, in order to heighten the wavelength and make it easier for him to hear words spoken from our dimension into his. I issued my instructions to him in clear incisive tones, and my Mentor then said,

'Tell him to see to it that all similar machines are checked,'

This too I passed on to the foreman, and to my gratification I heard him say, 'While you are at it, you'd better go over the other ones like this.' When they demurred he said, 'I'll answer for you; I'll not be held responsible for any accidents, and I'll tell them that; don't you worry.' And at this we were withdrawn from the scene, feeling we had left the situation in capable hands.

16

The Meeting of two Statesmen
(taken down approximately 1986)

The next mission I wish to describe is that of the meeting of two heads of state who represented two of the most powerful countries in the world. We were told that the forces of evil might not be present in visible form, for they were likely to depend on mental telepathy as a means of directing the issues in the way they wanted. In order to counteract their powerful beams we were to position ourselves closely about these men, thereby ensuring that God's higher electrical forces were surrounding and protecting them from the messages which would undoubtedly be directed at them by our enemy. *'When they find their lower beams are being deflected, their fury will know no bounds,'* we were told, *'so be forever on your guard both for yourself and for your neighbours.'*

Aware then as we were of the seriousness of the situation, we strengthened our resolve to fulfil our mission. As a precaution against an approach from behind we agreed to face in opposite directions, so that one might be directing his or her will on to the statesman nearest, or his advisers, and the next would be facing outwards to be ready to warn all of us should a member or members of the dark legion apopear in order to menace us.

No sooner had we stationed ourselves closely about these men, who conversed with the aid of interpreters, than we became aware of the by now familiar thrumming sensation incurred by the electrical forces at the disposal of the force of evil and which are slower and heavier than those used by God, so that to His children they can seem well nigh intolerable. Although we knew we could always cry to Him for help, we had been taught to withstand these forces as long as was endurable, for in this way more of the dark entities were attracted to the scene, and thus more of them were ultimately transported to their proper place, nevermore to return. At the same time we were adjured never to leave it too long, for fear we ourselves were overpowered and had not the strength to call to God for help.

In this instance we realized that the adverse conditions were worse than any we had previously encountered, and I found myself saying to the man who sat before me, 'Listen to the words of God only. Do not allow yourself to be beguiled by the precepts of the devil.' I repeated this and similar advice over and over again as forcefully as I could, although it seemed to require more and more of my will-power to continue doing it.

Suddenly my neighbour said, 'Look out, Jacques! They are here!'

Turning, I saw that we were encircled by dark, grotesque figures, who advanced menacingly towards us.

'Get back!' I shouted. 'Return to whence you came. In the name of God, I tell you to go.

I then uttered a quick prayer to God, asking for His help. As always the response was instan-taneous, for a stream of light was directed on to us from above, enveloping the entire scene. I believe the unearthly shrieks from the dark ones as they became transfixed by it, to their dismay, were heard even by some of the human beings, for I saw them turn and look about in some alarm. Seeing nothing amiss, however, in their own dimension, they resumed their work.

Although we had vanquished those dark entities sent to overpower us, nevertheless the powerful electrical forces were still being directed at us; in fact they seemed to gain in intensity so that it became hard to control our thoughts. I became alarmed, for already we had sought God's help and His light still shone around us, although it seemed to me that it had lost some of its brilliance and was in some way being fragmented by the terrible invisible force attacking us.

Just as I was about to appeal for help, my Mentor spoke. *'You have endured enough. We are going to replace you with a fresh team. Do not reproach yourselves. You have done well.'*

At once we found ourselves back in the Great Hall of the Citadel, receiving instructions to immerse ourselves immediately in cleansing waters to counteract the harmful rays to which we had been submitted.

I hurried to my Master's rooms and entering made my obeisance, at the same time warning him not to draw close to me, for I must first plunge into his pool. He seemed to know already, and nodded his approval.

Later, as we sat together on our customary seat, he explained the reason that I and my colleagues had been subjected to such a terrible onslaught was that the enemy, or force, of evil, recognized that now was their last chance of annihilating mankind, and if possible, the very planet; they were making their final bid to set nation against nation, and to that end they had made this determined effort to implant their inflammatory instructions into the minds of these statesmen, and equally so into the minds of their advisers, for these same advisers were not all men of integrity. Some of them had already been influenced beforehand and were apt to set their own interests first, or the interests of those whose vested interests they represented.

I understood well all that my Master told me, and was appalled by its implications, and yet I was not wholly satisfied by his explanation, for I remembered how even the power of God had seemed to wane at the renewed onslaught which we had undergone.

He answered me with slow deliberation. 'My child, hard though it may be for you to accept, it is a fact that this force of evil which opposes the Great One, your God, has at its disposal forces of such strength that they can, if concentrated upon a certain target, be even stronger than the Great One Himself.'

I looked at my Master aghast. 'But, my Master, we are taught that God is Lord of all. He is omnipotent. How can it be that the force of darkness is even stronger?'

'It is indeed a horrifying concept, my child, and yet it is one we must learn to accept. This force, known as the Destructive Force, is wholly alien to the Great One and to His children, and indeed to all of His creation. From whence it comes it is not thought fit that we should be told, nor its origin, for it is one of God's Mysteries, and one which we shall learn when we are sufficiently advanced on the path of evolution. As it is, we are told that it would be too horrifying and distressing for the Great One's children to know about, oppressed as they already are by this same force during their mortal lives. These indeed were not intended by Him to be led in so arduous, difficult and painful a way, and, were it not for the disobedience of Satanaku, mankind's passage through his earthly lives would have been of a very different nature.'

'How was it then, Master, that God did not reprimand Satan (as I have been led to call him), when he erred and defied commands?'

'Here, my child, we encounter one of the Laws of the Universe; namely, the law of freewill, to which even God Himself must adhere. Therefore, when this Archangel allowed himself to be taken over by the servants of the destructive force and to disobey God's will, owing to this same law of freewill he must be permitted to go his own way, even though the outcome would spell disaster both for mankind and for his environment.'

I found I could scarcely believe my ears, for though I trusted my Master's words implicitly yet what he said appeared to conflict with all the religious education I had received, and I sat in silence whilst my mind whirled in tumultuous confusion.

Finally my Master said, that he thought it advisable for me to rest for a while after my last and most trying confrontation of all, added to which was the shock of his startling revelations. He led me to the couch as before and, passing his hands briefly across my forehead, he made me sink into oblivion; such was the art of the early Egyptian Healer/Priests, I have since learnt.

When I returned to my senses I found him standing beside me. 'My child,' he said, 'you are to rejoin your group of comrades in the usual way, and with them you will go to a zone seldom visited by God's children for it is dark in the extreme, since all that is pertaining to it operates on that lowered force which is used by the evil ones who oppose the Great One in every way they can. The objective of you and your friends is to rescue as many of the denizens of this area as you are able, for they are indeed God's children, who have been led astray by the enemy; they continue to listen to their evil masters, who then use them as a means of trapping still more of God's children, ignorant as the majority are of the dangers of a life led unprotected by prayer. These for the most part are young unevolved entities who have not had the opportunity to learn God's ways, and who therefore are all the more easily led into lives of depravity and degradation, drawing others with them.'

I started up in horror on learning of these poor unfortunates, finding myself eager to attempt their rescue, but my Master laid a hand on my shoulder to delay me.

'You must constantly be aware of the great danger which you and your friends are running, for not only will you be bombarded by forces of almost intolerable strength but you will encounter the fury of the servants of the evil ones who brook no interference with their wicked plans.'

He then advised us to stand back to back, so that we could not be taken unawares; and, he said the best way to effect a rescue was to surround the one to whom we were directed and to impress on his or her mind that he should leave those dark realms, or the underworld, as he might well designate it, and he has only to give a single cry for help to God, and he will be taken to happier surroundings. Where there is obviously no belief in God, you can tell him that his friends and relations await him, but that they will never see him where he is, for they detest such dark unhealthy places. Go now, my child', said my Master; 'you will not be permitted to remain long in those dire regions, and on your return you must come straight to my sacred pool.'

He then accompanied me to the door of his apartment saying, as I bowed my farewell, 'May the Great One be ever close to you,' and I fancied I noted a tone of anxiety in his voice.

PART

3

In the Dark Realms

1

Avarice Holds a Soul Fast

I hurried to my place in the Great Hall, and I could tell by the serious expressions on my colleagues' faces that they too had been warned of the dangers before us.

My Mentor spoke: *'We are sending you first to a man who was possessed of great avarice on Earth, which led him to set his worldly wealth above all the humanities; but since the death of his physical self he has remained surrounded by his ledgers and the astral counterparts of the symbols of his wealth, counting and recounting them, and paying little heed to his dismal surroundings. Attempts have been made to turn his mind to other things, whereupon he will merely tries to strike a bargain, or to grant a loan greatly adventitious to himself, with God's messenger. We have reason to believe that he is at last tiring of his stalemate existence, and would respond to a suggestion of improving his lot. Your best hope is to remind him of his daughter, for whom he allowed himself some affection. Lily is her name. We dare not allow her to enter the dark regions, for she could not resist the prevailing forces.'*

At this, we found ourselves transported to the most appalling conditions I had yet experienced. Not only was it dark in that there was no apparent source of light, so that our surroundings could be observed only by the sort of luminosity to be found on a winter's night on Earth, but on every hand were dismal run-down buildings such as would be known as 'slums' on Earth. Figures of men and women loomed out of the gloom on either side, and on seeing us they shrieked obscenities and flung jibes at us, taunting us as they might have done agents of the law, in life. *'Turn into the house on your right,'* my Mentor said, *'and there you will find your man in what he considers to be his office.'*

We entered a dingy, looking house, as indeed they all were, and soon found our charge, for we could hear him muttering to himself, and when we went into the room we found him

173

shuffling papers and what appeared to be deeds about on his desk, whilst stacks more lay about it. The small room was lined with metal cupboards and it was dark in the extreme; indeed, this was the prime cause for his muttered complaints.

'How can I see to check my holdings, my lists and my accounts?' he cried. 'They've given me no light, and look at this miserable little room I have to make do for an office! I, who own several great mansions.'

Turning, he became aware of us and a fearful look came over his face. 'Who are you? Thieves, I've no doubt.' He clutched his papers to him, looking distrustfully at us.

'No, we are not thieves,' I said. 'We have come to help you. You must trust us.'

'Help me?' he exclaimed. 'Then can you take me to my own home? There is no light in this dreadful hole, and outside there are nothing but vagabonds and cheats.'

Tell him, my Mentor said, *'that this house is the replica of many he himself built on Earth in order to amass wealth for himself, and when his tenant, could not afford light he denied it them.'*

I passed on the messages, and he flew into a paroxysm of rage, expostulating on the unfairness and ridiculous implications of my words. I allowed him to vent his wrath, and then I said that he could indeed have light, and with it a better home to live in, if he consented to come with us.

At this he sprang to his feet and stepped towards the door, then halted where he stood. 'But I cannot leave all my wealth behind! Where would I be without it? You must help me take it', and he gathered up an armful of his precious deeds.

'You will have no use for them where we are going,' I told him. 'They belong to the earthly state, and have no worth in heaven.'

'In heaven!' exclaimed the poor wretch. 'D'you mean. .? Who are you? Angels? Are you telling me I'm dead?'

'We are not angels,' I replied, 'but messengers from God, and yes, you have left your mortal frame and are now in your heavenly form.'

He remained unconvinced and turned back to his desk, saying, 'I cannot leave my worldly wealth behind, the results of a lifetime's work.'

'Your daughter Lily wants you. She longs for you to be at her side once more.' His face softened for the first time, so I pressed home my point. 'She cares nothing for your wealth. She is happy and content where she is, but for the lack of the father she loved.'

'Then I must go to her. Show me where she is, for I long to see her. You will show me the way back here, won't you?' he added anxiously.

'You will be free to return here if you wish,' I said, and we noticed how the room had lightened already when the man had relented at the mention of his daughter.

Two of you will accompany him,' we were told; *'the rest will be transported to yet another case.'*

A column of light then enveloped the two who had stepped on either side of our charge, and then all three disappeared before our eyes.

---- **2** ----

Pride Holds a Soul Fast

We next found ourselves in a plain room, almost devoid of furnishings, which, for all its white walls and high windows, seemed clouded over with a film of darkness. At a prie–dieu a nun knelt in an attitude of prayer, but there was about her a stern, unbending look, which spoke of anything but the love of God.

'This Abbess has convinced herself that she alone is the interpreter of "Holy Writ", as she names it, and that all others fall short of her precepts. In life she was a stern, unfeeling Mother Superior, who liked to dominate and overpower all those about her; so much so that they came to dread her very presence; and, instead of instilling love into their hearts, into their relationships with the other members of their order, and with outsiders, her regime was so harsh and cold that it reflected itself throughout the convent. Now she cannot accept the reality of her death, for she had a preconceived idea of 'heaven', whereas all she can see about her is the cold sterility of the cell she occupied in life, while if she ventures beyond it she merely finds the dark and hostile region which you have just witnessed yourselves. Go to her, and suggest to her that she prays to God that His love may reach out and show her the course her life should take now.'

We gathered round this poor deluded woman, and one by one we spoke to her.

At first she expressed great indignation at the invasion of her privacy. 'No one may enter my room without being summoned by me,' she said, 'not even Sister Angela, the sub–Abbess. Nor do I allow men in my convent,' she added, looking angrily at those of us who were manifesting in male incarnations. 'You will leave at once.' She confronted us with looks almost amounting to hatred.

176

'Tell her you are messengers from God,' my Mentor said.

I stepped closer to her and said gently, 'We come not as intruders but as messengers from God, for He longs to have you nearer to Him and not shut in this lonely cell.'

She turned on me with scorn. 'I need no messenger to tell me how to reach our Heavenly Father! I pray to Him continuously, and it is I who teach others how to reach Him. Was I not at prayer when you interrupted me?'

'But do you hear His answer, Lady Abbess?' I asked her, and I observed a slight flinch before she replied, 'Who are you to question me as to my faith?'

'I repeat: I am His messenger, and I only wish you well, for you have reached a new phase in your existence, and we have been sent to show you how best to lead it.'

At this she turned sharply to me. 'A new phase! Explain yourself. Am I to be promoted to a place more suited to my long experience and years of service?'

Her arrogance was daunting, and I left a colleague to answer this, knowing her to be more patient than I.

'Indeed God has work for you to do, and indeed it will be in yet another place,' said my colleague gently; 'for you have finished with this place, as you have finished with that last earth–life to which you refer. If you come with us, we shall take you to your new home, and then you will be told what it is that God wishes you to learn.'

'I, learn!' exclaimed the Abbess indignantly. 'It is *I* who teach.'

'Who is there here for you to teach?' I asked her, and again I saw her flinch, and realised that I had made my point. 'Come, let us pray to God that He will send His guiding light, that you may indeed find your promotion to those heavenly realms which are now to be your home.'

Before she could protest any further I said aloud a prayer to God for His protecting light, and on the instant a ray of light illuminated that clouded, dingy room. The Abbess' astonishment was such that she appeared quite overcome, and complied quite willingly when the two who had been instructed stepped forward and, taking her hands, led her away from that dark region; the rest of us saw them no more. By her very compliance with them she had released herself from her sterile bondage to which she had condemned herself for many Earth years.

3

A Gambler's Hell

There were now six of us left, and we found ourselves transported to a very different scene. Here we were in a gambling, house, where could be seen every kind of game of chance in progress. The players looked intent on their game to the extent that they were unaware of all that went on about them. The hall was dark in the extreme, and several voices called for lights to be brought, (although no one ever answered them, for there is never any light in that dark region.)

'There is a man here who has grown heartily tired of this endless round of games in which he is trying to score off his neighbours. He sees no way of escape, for they only haul him back to the table with threats and oaths if he attempts to go. He sits by that empty fireplace, where he and his companions are throwing dice. Go to him, and try to find a way of freeing him from the life he once enjoyed but now abhors.'

At once we recognised this poor unfortunate, for it was evident that his heart was not in the game, and he cast despairing glances about him as though looking for a means of escape.

All at once he seemed to see us, and we drew near and stood encircling his group. I, remembering my Master's advice, positioned myself with my back to one of my colleagues, and I observed the others taking the same precaution. One of our number facing inwards became the spokesman.

'Are you not tired of this endless game?' she asked. 'We can take you away to a happier place than this. You have only to ask us.'

His response was instantaneous, for he jumped to his feet saying, 'Yes, I'd give anything to get away from here, – and these cheating rogues,' he added injudiciously. An uproar ensued as the other men protested violently that they were not cheats, but on the contrary he was the one who was swindling them. The noise was such that gamblers from all parts of the hall turned to look, and they too shouted insults. Pandemonium broke out, and our man implored us to take him away, but immediately the man on his right sprang up shouting, 'Oh no, you're not going. You owe me, my stake. Give it to me or I'll give you this,' and he pulled out a wicked, looking knife.

'I've got no money of yours,' protested our poor unfortunate, whereupon the villain stabbed him where on Earth would have been his heart.

To the amazement of all the onlookers the dagger dropped harmlessly to the floor, and our man remained standing where he was.

'You cannot kill him,' I said, 'for he is already dead, as are you yourself, and indeed are all these others', and I swept my arm around the scene. 'Nor is money of any use to you, once you are dead, and the sooner you all realize that, the better. This is no place for children of God. Ask that you be taken to higher realms.'

Whilst I had been speaking the intolerable forces used by the evil ones had been growing stronger and stronger, so that I found it difficult to think or speak, and now I became aware of those by now all-too-familiar dark forms emerging from shadowy recesses and closing in on us. I tried to avoid their hypnotic eyes and hideous leers.

'Take your charge by the hands. We are removing you at once,' my Mentor said; *'you have done well, not only in rescuing him, but by implanting in the minds of others their true situation. That was why you met with such a barrage of opposition from the enemy.'*

At once we found ourselves back in the Citadel, and the relief to be freed from the unbearable jarring of the forces used against us was tremendous. I hurried to my Master's rooms and on entering found he was already in his garden.

'Come, my son, you must immerse yourself at once. You have been subjected to as severe a force as is to be borne by one of God's children, and the shock is bad for you.'

He hurried on ahead and then stood aside as I plunged myself into the cool, soothing water in his garden.

When I emerged I asked him anxiously, 'But, my Master, where is he whom we would rescue? I did not see him amongst our number in the Citadel, and yet he had appealed to us for help.' I felt most distressed to think we might have left him under those appalling circumstances.

'Calm yourself, my child, for he is safe. His very request to be removed made it possible for him to leave the dark regions forever. His own Guides are caring for him. He could not accompany you to so high a plane as the Citadel, for he is not evolved enough. He would have seen nothing, and would have felt an insecurity almost as bad as that of the dark realms. He is with his own kind now, where he will learn his rightful place in the scheme of things.'

Great was my relief on hearing this, and I took my place on the seat beside my Master, and described to him all that had taken place since last I saw him.

EPLIOGUE

Having given these examples of the missions on which a novice and an initiated Knight are sent, I shall now sum up my experiences by saying that these missions are carried out continuously by The Company of White Knights in order to combat the wicked forces which oppose the will of God in every way they are able, and on every plane of existence.

I wish to thank my scribe, to whom I have dictated this book: she, who was to have been my sister in this her present life, had not I and our mother died upon my re–entry into the world, and who now has the almost equally formidable task of finding a publisher for it.

Jacques.